G000048221

Opening up
Ecclesiastes

JIM WINTER

DayOne

Opening up
Ecclesiastes

JIM WINTER

'Ecclesiastes is a book which has both puzzled and repelled many a reader, and even caused not a few to question its place in the biblical canon. Dr. Winter's approach persuasively establishes its unique place within inspired Scripture, and uncovers its special relevance to our own troubled times. His work on Ecclesiastes provides faithful, informed exposition, and sensitive and relevant application. His style is straightforward and engaging throughout, and the format, promoting follow-up study and discussion, is a further strength. It is a pleasure to commend this exposition to a wide readership.'

Bruce Milne,
Former Senior Minister, First Baptist Church, Vancouver

'For millions of people, the Preacher's opening salvo in Ecclesiastes sums up their experience of life: 'Meaningless!' Life lived only on the horizontal plane, 'under the sun', as he puts it, is really empty and futile. In this competent guide to this often misunderstood and misquoted book, Jim Winter, by means of reliable interpretation, apt illustrations and judicious quotes, repeatedly points us to life above the horizontal, to 'life in the Son'. Like me, you will find here a book to inform the mind, warm the heart and challenge the will to live a life with real 'Meaning'—life in Christ!'

Dr Steve Brady

Principal, Moorlands College, Christchurch

© Day One Publications 2005

First printed 2005

Scripture quotations are from the New King James Version,
Thomas Nelson Publishers, 1983

ISBN 1 903087 86 -4

9 781903 087862

British Library Cataloguing in Publication Data available

Published by Day One Publications
Ryelands Road, Leominster, HR6 8NZ
Telephone 01568 613 740   FAX 01568 611 473

email—sales@dayone.co.uk
web site—www.dayone.co.uk
North American—e-mail-sales@dayonebookstore.com

Designed by Steve Devane and printed by Gutenberg Press, Malta

To my grandchilden:
Samuel, Luke, Hanna, Ben and Joshua

List of Bible abbreviations

THE OLD TESTAMENT		1 Chr.	1 Chronicles	Dan.	Daniel
		2 Chr.	2 Chronicles	Hosea	Hosea
Gen.	Genesis	Ezra	Ezra	Joel	Joel
Exod.	Exodus	Neh.	Nehemiah	Amos	Amos
Lev.	Leviticus	Esth.	Esther	Obad.	Obadiah
Num.	Numbers	Job	Job	Jonah	Jonah
Deut.	Deuteronomy	Ps.	Psalms	Micah	Micah
Josh.	Joshua	Prov.	Proverbs	Nahum	Nahum
Judg.	Judges	Eccles.	Ecclesiastes	Hab.	Habakkuk
Ruth	Ruth	S.of.S.	Song of Solomon	Zeph.	Zephaniah
1 Sam.	1 Samuel	Isa.	Isaiah	Hag.	Haggai
2 Sam.	2 Samuel	Jer.	Jeremiah	Zech.	Zechariah
1 Kings	1 Kings	Lam.	Lamentations	Mal.	Malachi
2 Kings	2 Kings	Ezek.	Ezekiel		

THE NEW TESTAMENT		Gal.	Galatians	Heb.	Hebrews
		Eph.	Ephesians	James	James
Matt.	Matthew	Phil.	Philippians	1 Peter	1 Peter
Mark	Mark	Col.	Colossians	2 Peter	2 Peter
Luke	Luke	1 Thes.	1 Thessalonians	1 John	1 John
John	John	2 Thes.	2 Thessalonians	2 John	2 John
Acts	Acts	1 Tim.	1 Timothy	3 John	3 John
Rom.	Romans	2 Tim.	2 Timothy	Jude	Jude
1 Cor.	1 Corinthians	Titus	Titus	Rev.	Revelation
2 Cor.	2 Corinthians	Philem.	Philemon		

Overview

Taxi drivers like to boast about the famous people they carry in their cabs. One such driver once remarked, 'I had the philosopher, Bertrand Russell, in my cab the other day. I said to him, "Bertie! What's it all about then?" Do you know, the silly beggar couldn't tell me!'

From time to time everyone pauses and asks, 'What is the meaning of life?' For some, it is only a momentary thing—but others want to probe more deeply into the question. It is an uncomfortable pursuit as it brings us face to face with reality and mortality.

When things are going well, we may easily evade the question, absorbing ourselves in our day-to-day activities—filling the gaps with entertaining diversions—making the most of the time we have allocated to us.

On occasions of sickness, national disaster or bereavement, the question comes back to us and we pause a little longer—trying to make sense of the seeming futility that lies before us—before getting back on track and evading the issue until the next time it is thrust upon us!

The writer of Ecclesiastes, however, does not run away from the problem—he faces it boldly—devoting much time to its study. His conclusions strike a chord in the heart of modern people and point us to the true meaning and purpose of life.

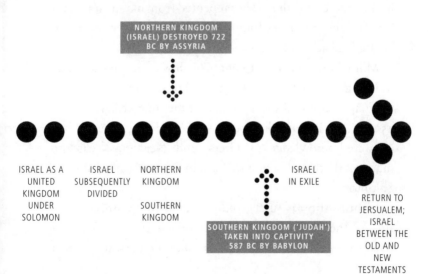

NORTHERN KINGDOM (ISRAEL) DESTROYED 722 BC BY ASSYRIA

ISRAEL AS A UNITED KINGDOM UNDER SOLOMON

ISRAEL SUBSEQUENTLY DIVIDED

NORTHERN KINGDOM

SOUTHERN KINGDOM

ISRAEL IN EXILE

SOUTHERN KINGDOM ('JUDAH') TAKEN INTO CAPTIVITY 587 BC BY BABYLON

RETURN TO JERSUALEM; ISRAEL BETWEEN THE OLD AND NEW TESTAMENTS

OPENING UP ECCLESIASTES

Background and summary

Who and when?

Ecclesiastes is the Greek equivalent of the Hebrew word *Qoheleth*, used in the Septuagint, the Greek translation of the Old Testament. In the New Testament, *Ecclesia* is used as a title for God's assembled people—the *church*. Ecclesiastes literally means *leader of the assembly* and has been given English equivalents including, teacher, president, speaker, professor and pundit. In this book he will be known as the Preacher—the title used in the NKJV.

He describes himself as, 'the son of David, king in Jerusalem' (1:1, *cf.* 1.12). Our natural conclusion is that he is Solomon (about 971-931 B.C.), writing towards the end of his life, indicating that he has repented from his apostasy and turned back to God—although there is no evidence of this in the biblical account of his life (1 Kings 1-11).

Many evangelical commentators, however, question this, pointing out that the style of the book, and some of the language employed would date it at the time of Ezra (about 450 B.C.). It has also been suggested that the author exhibited knowledge of Greek and Near East wisdom material that would not have been in existence at the time of Solomon.

Identification is further complicated by the theory that this is the work of more than one author—a kind of narrator—using the material of another person to great effect.

These things should not trouble us unduly, and will certainly not affect our understanding of its meaning, for the contents of the book clearly show that it is written from Solomon's *perspective*. In this guide, we will refer to the author as Solomon. The Preacher, like Israel's third king, is a man of great wisdom, and has studied the meaning of life and carefully presents his conclusions to his readers (12:9-10).

Why?

What place does this book have in the Bible? Many have asked this question in the light of its pessimism and humanistic sentiments. Primarily it acts as a foil or contrast to the other books. It is 'a brilliant, artful argument for the way one would look at life—*if* God did *not* play a direct, intervening role in life and *if* there were no life after death.' [1]

The Book of Ecclesiastes often reads like the diary of despair, sometimes portraying life as a sick joke, with death as the punch line—full of what one writer has called 'cynical wisdom'—mostly directing the reader to the meaninglessness of life, yet sometimes urging him to make the most of it, and even—in the end—instructing him to 'Fear God and keep his commandments'. His journey towards that conclusion is sometimes tortuous as he honestly

> He never abandons his belief in a Sovereign Creator God who, in the end, is the Master of his destiny. The glimpses the author gives us 'above the sun' shine out of the gloom of his materialistic conclusions.

grapples with the evidence that lies before him 'under the sun'—yet he never abandons his belief in a Sovereign Creator God who, in the end, is the Master of his destiny. The glimpses the author gives us 'above the sun' shine out of the gloom of his materialistic conclusions.

How?

In June 1942, Oscar Schindler inadvertently witnessed an Aktion in the Krakow ghetto in Poland. These were Nazi attacks to round up Jews for deportation to the death camps. They were meticulously planned and usually the Nazis were assisted by collaborators. At the time, Schindler and his mistress were out for a pleasant horseback ride on a hilltop when the Aktion opened directly below them. Astonished by the Nazi ferocity, Schindler's eye was drawn to a little girl dressed in red who, alone, stood out from the mass of Jews being herded to the trains and to their death. Many years later Schindler looked back on this event and said, 'Beyond this day, no thinking person could fail to see what would happen. I was now resolved to do everything in my power to defeat the system.'

A notorious womanizer and lover of the 'good life', he had amassed a fortune through bribery and corruption, exploiting every opportunity that his status as a member of the Nazi party presented. In the light of what he saw, the 'good life' became meaningless! He went on to risk his life and spend a fortune—dying penniless—in the rescue of an estimated twelve hundred Jews in the shadow of Auschwitz.

When Steven Spielberg retold the story in *Schindler's List*, the main body of the film was shot in black and white, except for the glow of candles and the two scenes in which the girl in the red coat appears, picked out in colour. The effect was both stunning and heartbreaking as she stood out from the mass of humanity that was being herded to their deaths. Later in the film we see the girl in the red coat again, as her body, along with 10,000 Jews killed in the Nazi massacres, is exhumed and burned.

Ecclesiastes is life portrayed in black and white, emphasizing the captivity and destruction of a whole race—the human race— gathered together under the shadow of death. But there is colour. The occasional candle flickers and soon others begin to glow and illuminate the scene. The brightest colour appears when the cameras focus upon one person vividly illuminated against the drab back-drop— not a little girl in a red coat, but God, the Creator of human beings. As the camera pans away and the span of biblical history is revealed, we see that same God among the seething mass of humanity, sharing in their suffering and death— Jesus Christ.

The book that portrays the pointlessness of everything really does have a point to make!

1 The Preacher

(1:1-11)

The Preacher is well qualified to search for the meaning of life—exploring many avenues of human experience and leaving no stone unturned in his quest.

After introducing himself (v. 1), the Preacher introduces his text (v. 2), and what follows is his exposition and conclusion. The rest of the book explains how and why he has come to this conclusion.

'You can quote me on that' (v. 2)

Throughout time, people have been aware of the power of words. A rousing, impassioned speech has often changed the course of events—a book has changed the course of history—and even an impromptu remark has enhanced or diminished someone's reputation. Such things are sometimes the result of momentary inspiration, but often they are the products of careful deliberation. Winston Churchill's wartime speeches and broadcasts were peppered with phrases that would express and inspire the resolve of the British people in their fight against Nazi tyranny. We now know how carefully rehearsed they were.

It appears that the Preacher has thought long and hard over this matter and uses a phrase that will precisely and concisely put over his message. It is as if he is saying, 'Here is my point and you can quote me on that!' This phrase, *vanity of vanities,* is used many times within Ecclesiastes; and the singular, *vanity*, frequently occurs in the Old Testament. The employment and repetition of this term stresses the importance of what the Preacher is saying. To understand his argument fully, we must look further into the meaning of this word.

The vanity of vanity

The Hebrew translated as 'vanity' is *hebel*, which literally means 'breeze, breath or vapour'. It is used in a number of ways in the Old Testament and these give us an all-round picture of what the Preacher is telling us about the meaninglessness of life under the sun.

Vanity in relation to time

Hebel speaks of the transitory nature of things. It is used in this way in the Psalms, where human life is described as 'a vapour' (Ps. 39:5, 11). Derek Kidner likens it to, 'A wisp of vapour, a puff of wind, a mere breath—nothing you could get your hands on; the nearest thing to zero.' [1] Everything in an earthbound life is fleeting. It is utterly futile to try to hold on to anything, for, in the end, all will burst like a bubble and be taken from us. Jesus reinforces this when he refers to 'treasures on earth' (Matt. 6:19).

Vanity in relation to value

The Psalmist also uses the same word for that which is false and worthless. 'Therefore their days he consumed in futility... The LORD knows the thoughts of man, that they are futile (Ps. 78:33; 94:11). Jeremiah also takes up the theme, when he speaks of 'worthlessness and unprofitable things' (Jer. 16:19). Many things of this world have a habit of disappointing us. They only flatter to deceive. We may invest our lives pursuing things that at first seem almost priceless, only to discover that we have been wasting our time in pointless activity. It is vanity because such time is irretrievable—lost for ever.

Vanity in relation to eternity

Hebel is also used in reference to idols. Jeremiah employs the term in this context (Jer. 10:8,14). Idols will consume our interest—even become our gods—keeping us from the one true God. They can take many forms other than material objects crafted by man. We may idolize our children or grandchildren, friends, careers, homes, our ambitions and dreams.

> Some things appear to have great value when we first pursue them, but having got hold of them we realize that they are worthless and we regret the time we wasted on them.

We can sum vanity up in the following way: some things may be of value to us; but they are vanity because we will not always have them. At any time, without warning, they can be taken from us. Some things appear to have great value when we first pursue them, but having got hold of them we realize that they are worthless and we regret the time we wasted on them. Some things have become like idols. We value them above all else, they remain with us all our days, but we have to leave them behind only to discover, too late, that they have kept us from God.

Absolute vanity

'Vanity of vanities' is an expression of the absolute. Nothing exceeds the vanity that the Preacher has discovered in his search for the meaning of a life without God. This method of repeating a word is used elsewhere in the Bible for the same purpose (Exod. 26:33; Gen. 9:25; Deut. 10:14; 1 Tim. 6:15).

The Preacher refers to everything as being vanity. Although there is no specific reference at this point in his text, he will later explain that he is referring to everything that is subject to the temporal restrictions of life, under the sun. Without the Creator, the whole of creation is subject to futility (Rom. 8:20). Charles Bridges calls it, 'one vast heap of numberless perishing vanities.' [2]

The unanswerable question (vv. 3-10)

The Bible presents secularized man with some powerful, probing questions (Mark 8:36-37; Heb. 2:3; Job 25:4). Here the Preacher introduces another recurring phrase, *under the sun*. This maps out the territory in which his search for the meaning and purpose of life takes place. The term is unique to the Preacher although it is synonymous with the expression, 'under heaven', found elsewhere in the Old Testament (Exod. 17:14; Deut. 7:24; 9:14). His use of it gives hope to the reader, for it strongly implies that there is an area in which life is not meaningless—above the sun! He mentions four areas of investigation.

Filling in time (v. 4)

Here is life in relation to its natural human span. We live in a world that is manifesting the effects of pollution on a vast scale. Scientists speak of impending disaster in terms of hundreds of years, whereas, not long ago, they were speculating in millions. In the context of eternity, the world itself is just another fleeting object subject to the ravages of sin. Yet, as the Preacher observes, compared to the world, man's life is merely a whisper! The earth seems to be the one permanent thing in all of existence—yet everything born upon it will soon be gone and replaced by its successor. He thinks of past generations, which were here just a moment ago and are gone. Soon he will join them and be replaced by his successors who will be replaced by . . . and so it goes on. We were not here when most of the great events in history occurred; and we will not be here to witness its future outworking. If this is so, what then is the purpose of it all? Surely, it is totally meaningless.

What goes round, comes round (vv. 5-7)

The Preacher now looks at life as it relates to the natural world. His previous description of meaninglessness was linear. He saw people's lives as a series of straight lines of which his would eventually come to a halt while others carried on. Now he thinks in terms of a circle on which his own life exists, but will eventually be thrown off into oblivion! He arrives at this conclusion by observing the cycle of the natural world. What goes round, comes round—but one day he will not be here to see it! The intricate patterns of the cycle of nature declare the glory of God (Ps. 19:1), but mock the atheist—these things declare the meaninglessness of his life. It is interesting to note how the Preacher uses the sun, wind and rivers as his metaphors of meaninglessness. In other passages of Scripture they are used to describe the joy and hope to be found in God. (Mal. 4:2; John 8:12; 3:8; 7:38).

No satisfaction (v. 8)

This idea of labour follows on from the Preacher's previous observations. Everything, under the sun, is laborious—nothing is completed to man's satisfaction. This idea of the eye not being satisfied with seeing, nor the ear with hearing sums up the spirit of our own age. Technology advances so quickly that most things are 'state of the art' for only a matter of weeks. Yet millions of people are trying to find satisfaction in the materialistic world—with the futile expectation that behind the obvious benefits of material things there lurks some hidden greater joy. In this context Jean-Paul Sartre was right when he commented, 'Things are entirely what they appear to be and behind them . . . there is nothing'.[3] This is graphically true for those who are limited to an 'under the sun' perspective. Contentment or satisfaction never comes to those who are caught up in this cycle. The Bible speaks of satisfaction for those whose vision extends beyond the temporal into the eternal (Phil. 4:11-13).

Those who, in Jesus Christ, have had the veil lifted realize that material things are our servants and not our masters (Prov. 15:16).

The cycle of sameness (vv. 9-10)

The Preacher can also see vanity repeated in history. 'History is going nowhere,' says one commentator and, 'like the earth, appears to change, but in actuality it stays the same. Nothing new ever happens.' 4 He is right. The modern world gives every indication of advancement, but flatters to deceive. New technology enables us to do the same things in a different way, or, at least, a little more quickly! At its best it can alleviate suffering and prolong life for a little longer—at its worst it enables man to inflict greater suffering upon greater numbers with less effort! In between, it achieves very little. We have labour-saving devices and we can now travel faster and further than our forefathers, yet do we achieve more than they did?

At this point the Preacher appears to have abandoned the life philosophy of his forefathers. For them, history had a redemptive goal and purpose—not the sad cycle of sameness of the godless philosopher. Karl Marx sadly expressed their exasperation when he said, 'History repeats itself, first as a tragedy, then as a farce.' 5 The apostle Peter warns the church that in the last days this way of thinking will still be prevalent (2 Peter 3:3-4). In 'under the sun' thinking, there can be nothing new. But the Bible teaches that history is controlled by a God who will make all things new (Rev. 21:5); whose mercies are new every morning (Lam. 3:23); who gives his people new hearts (Ezek. 36:26), and puts a new song in them

(Isa. 42:10). It is a man or woman who has an eye for the eternal who sees the hand of God within the temporal.

In loving memory? (v. 11)

The world remembers notable people—but most of us will be soon forgotten. The Bible, however, gives a different picture—no one is forgotten. Every person, along with every remembered thought and deed, will one day stand before God (2 Tim. 4:1). Those who have entered into a living relationship with him through his Son, Jesus Christ, will know that their names are written in the book of life (Rev. 21:27), and engraved upon the palms of his hand (Isa. 49:16). Those who have rejected him will face his judgement in condemnation (Rom. 3:19)—but no one will be forgotten!

The Preacher is right, but he is only half right. What he says is true—but it is only true in a limited sense. Jesus gives us the whole picture: 'Whoever desires to come after me, let him deny himself, and take up his cross, and follow me. For whoever desires to save his life will lose it, but whoever loses his life for my sake and the gospel's will save it. For what will it profit a man if he gains the whole world, and loses his own soul? Or what will a man give in exchange for his soul?' (Mark 8:34-37). He also speaks of the folly of those who seek their treasures solely on earth, and do not take on the eternal perspective by seeking treasures in heaven (Matt. 6:19-21).

For further study ▶

FOR FURTHER STUDY

1. Read Matthew 6:19-34 and Mark 8:34-38. Can you see the contrast between 'under the sun' thinking and a true biblical perspective on life?

2. Look for the word 'vanity' and note the way in which the Preacher uses it in his book.

TO THINK ABOUT AND DISCUSS

1. What do you make of the Preacher so far? Is he a man who has fully embraced the humanistic thinking of his day? Or is he writing from another perspective?

2. List your priorities. What are the things that take up most of your time? Which are the most valuable? Are you allocating the right amount of time to each one according to its value?

2 "Tis folly to be wise'

(1:12-18 and 2:12-16)

The Preacher takes us into his specific areas of investigation. His first step is into an area that separates man most from the animal kingdom—wisdom. This will be both the instrument with which he studies his subject, and also a field of investigation in itself.

Knowing the history of Solomon, it is not surprising that wisdom takes the prominent place in his pursuit of meaning. The Hebrew word he uses has been interpreted by one scholar as, 'endowed with reason and using it. . . wise from experience of life, and skilful with regard to affairs both human and divine.' [1] From Solomon's perspective, wisdom ought to be an end in itself. But we shall see even wisdom has its tragic limitations!

The Preacher's credentials (1:12-13)

When we pick up a book, it is helpful to know the

qualifications and background of the writer. If anyone has the credentials to write this book, then Solomon is our man!

His position (v. 12)

He was the son of David and he was gifted by God with great wisdom (1 Kings 3:9-12). His wisdom was put to the test in the story of the two harlots (1 Kings 3:16-28). He was the author and collector of wisdom literature—the books of Proverbs and Song of Songs are attributed to him—and he is reputed to have written over one thousand songs, although only two are included in the book of Psalms (Ps. 72 and 127).

His wealth

Solomon was rich beyond measure. Although his wealth was a gift from God (1 Kings 3:13), like many before him and since, it contributed to his downfall. By using the strategic location of his kingdom, he was able to monopolize one of the most important trade routes of his day (1 Kings 10:28-29). With an entrepreneurial spirit he secured an alliance with the Phoenicians in maritime trade, opening an important port at Elath on the Gulf of Akabah (1 Kings 9:26-28). Silver was 'as common in Jerusalem as stones' (1 Kings 10:27). He adopted a luxurious lifestyle in keeping with his success, building a palace for himself and his seven hundred wives and three hundred concubines. Compared to him, even the most affluent of today's high flyers would seem like paupers! Even Jesus spoke of him in this context when, referring to the lilies of the field, he said, 'Even Solomon in all his glory was not arrayed like one of these' (Matt. 6:29).

His leadership

Solomon had a chequered career as a leader. During his reign, there was little conflict between Israel and the surrounding nations. This was mostly due to alliances he formed through his marriages to foreign women from important families. Most notably, he married Pharaoh's daughter, thus forging a link between Israel and Egypt (1 Kings 3:1). He also became an ally of Hiram, king of Tyre (1 Kings 5:1-12). This enabled him to conduct his sea trade in union with the Phoenicians, but it also brought great unrest at home through the pledging of twenty Galilaean cities in return for aid (1 Kings 9:10, 11). Under his administration, traditional tribal boundaries were replaced by the introduction of taxation districts (1 Kings 4:7). However, resentment soon arose in the nation as he began to recruit his own people as conscripted labourers to carry out his ambitious building projects.

His interests

He was an expert in natural history. The plant named after him, Solomon's seal, is said to have the symbol of the Star of David at its roots, and its flowers were used as a love-potion. He was also regarded as a worker of magic. He enjoyed a high standing among occult practitioners in the Middle Ages. The *Clavicula Salomonis*, or Key of Solomon, an alchemical and occult book attributed to him, was one of the most influential and important textbooks for mediaeval magicians. It has been translated into many languages and still sells widely among new-age adherents today.

In modern humanistic terms we could describe him as 'the

man who had everything'. He was the ultimate celebrity, with charisma, wealth and power and this was coupled with a kind of pluralistic spirituality that made him acceptable to everyone.

His magnum opus

How then can a book so despairing of the world's plaudits be attributed to him? The answer can only be adequately arrived at when we examine his relationship with God. His greatest work was the building of the temple that was so dear to his father David's heart. His prayer of dedication shows us that here was a man of great spirituality who knew and loved God (1 Kings 8:22-53). Yet he broke the covenant he had with God as he sought to syncretize all the religions he had brought into his household through intermarriage. For the sake of political expediency and possibly for other reasons, he wilfully disobeyed God's command not to intermarry (1 Kings 11:2). This inevitably turned his heart from the Lord to their gods (1 Kings 11:4).

His wisdom (1:13)

How better to begin his pursuit than with the most profound of human qualities, and in an area in which he is familiar— *wisdom*. As a man gifted with wisdom and as a collector of wise sayings, he has the means by which he can thoroughly investigate the meaning and purpose of life. Or so he thinks! He will discover, as he goes more deeply into his subject, that the instrument of his investigation will ultimately be used to mock him and bring him to despair when he uncovers the futility of life without God. A man's most god-like qualities can only bring misery to a godless life!

His perseverance (1:13)

We cannot accuse him of treating his subject lightly. He speaks here of a devotion to his pursuit of meaning and purpose. He has set his heart on his endeavours. The words, 'seek and search' show the extent of the Preacher's investigations. He approaches the subject on two levels.

We can illustrate his method in the following way. If we were to make a study of a particular drug, in the way that the Preacher studies the meaning of life, we would have to do two things. Firstly, we would need to make a theoretical appraisal. Tests would have to be undertaken. We would gather information from patients' records to discover possible side effects. A long-term strategy of research would have to be implemented and satisfactory conclusions would have to be reached before the drug were made available to the public. Secondly, we would take the drug and experience its effects for ourselves!

His burden

He describes the whole process as a 'grievous task'. Not only is man exhausting himself in pointless exploration, it is God who has set him this very task! It would seem that here is the treadmill of hopelessness, made by God, on which man is wearying himself. Is there anything positive to say at this point? Yes, there is. For this is the very place where futility can be replaced by faith. This is pictured in the parable of the two sons (Luke 15:11-32). The lost son explores life and finds himself helplessly ensnared by the world. It is here that he comes to his senses, realizes what he has lost, and sets his sights once more on his father's house. This, for so many, is a God-ordained place of repentance and faith.

The Preacher's confession (1:14-18)

In this section, the Preacher reintroduces two of his sayings, *under the sun* and *vanity*. He also introduces a third, *grasping for the wind*. These words sum up what he is trying to say about the futility of life without God. He introduces a proverb to strengthen and expand what he is saying in the previous verse. This is in the true Solomonic tradition. We do not know whether this is of his own authorship or one that has been gleaned from another source, but it aptly suits his purpose. 'What is crooked cannot be made straight, and what is lacking cannot be numbered' (v. 15). Under the sun, as Michael Eaton says, 'There are twists and gaps in all thinking.'[2] The first part of this proverb has a parallel later on in the book. 'Consider the work of God; for who can make straight what he has made crooked?' (Eccles 7:13). If we try to discover the meaning of life and, in the process, leave God out of the equation, our conclusion will be distorted and illusionary. To do so means that we are left with a distorted conclusion that cannot be straightened until God is put back into the equation. As a consequence, our conclusion has no substance.

> If we ... leave God out of the equation, our conclusion will be distorted and illusionary.

The Preacher pauses before proceeding to another proverb (vv. 16-17). Again, he uses the term, *grasping for the wind* to describe the ever-growing frustration and futility of his quest.

His second proverb can be summed up by the more commonly used quotation from Thomas Gray: 'Where ignorance is bliss, 'tis folly to be wise.' Knowledge in itself can never make us happy. In the first place it is insatiable, and its increase only heightens the awareness of our ignorance. Secondly, it heightens our awareness of sin. Jesus said, 'If I had not come and spoken to them, they would have no sin, but now they have no excuse for their sin' (John 15:22). As the Puritan, Thomas Watson, remarked, 'How unprofitable is the luxuriancy of knowledge? He who is only filled with knowledge is like a glass filled with froth. What a vain, foolish thing it is to have knowledge and make no spiritual use of it.' 3

The author's comparison (2:12-16)

Although this section of Ecclesiastes is separated from the previous one by eleven verses, it, in a sense, completes, or rounds it off (v. 12). After the despair of what went on before, he appears to have more positive thoughts. We soon see, however, that these are quickly dashed.

Hopeful thoughts (vv. 13-14)

He compares wisdom and folly with light and darkness. There is a sense in which he is perfectly right to do this. The Bible does it, too. Jesus Christ, the Wisdom of God personified (1 Cor. 1:30), said, 'I am the light of the world. He who follows me shall not walk in darkness, but have the light of life' (John 8:12). As we increase in knowledge, and have the wisdom to use it in the right way, we are more able to understand the complexities of life under the sun. Through the study of philosophy, sociology and psychology, man is more able to understand his own nature. He is able to look at his behaviour and address its idiosyncrasies and imperfections. The only trouble is that he is unable to do anything to change them! It is here that comparison helps deal with the pain of reality. Secular man counts wisdom as enlightenment. It is interesting to note that elsewhere in the Bible, when these two things are compared, a different conclusion is reached. The apostle Paul speaks of the wisdom of God and the foolishness of man (1 Cor. 1:20-25)!

Doubtful thoughts (v. 14)

The word translated as, 'event' is elsewhere rendered as, 'fate' (NIV). Although the context naturally leads us to understand this as a reference to death, we must bear in mind that the Hebrew has a broader meaning. It refers to 'things that happen', both good and bad. It reminds us that both the wise man and the fool are subject to the events that happen in their lives. Each individual's fate is in the hands of Almighty God. Wisdom may enable a man to cope successfully with the problems presented by life, but unless it is true godly wisdom he will be confounded when faced with 'the law of sin and death' (Rom. 8:2).

Dreadful thoughts (vv. 15-16)

Death is the great leveller that awaits all men. For the materialist, the only hope of any kind of immortality is in the monuments or achievements that are left behind. But even these ultimately mock him—for who, in the end, takes any notice of them? Gordon Keddie sums it up well, when he writes, 'Death is the wall that under-the-sun secularism cannot climb. Even the remembrance of those who have died perishes with those who knew them personally. Beethoven may be said to live on in his music, but the truth is we know the music, not the man.' 4

Sadly, the Preacher has failed at the very beginning of his pursuit for meaning and purpose to life 'under the sun'. He has played his ace, wisdom, and even that has been beaten. Modern man repeats this tragedy, and will continue to do so until he realizes that God holds all the trump cards.

FOR FURTHER STUDY

1. Read through the life of Solomon to get a clearer picture of the man (1 Kings 1-11).
2. Notice how the apostle Paul compares the wisdom of God and the wisdom of man (1 Cor. 1:18-2:16).

TO THINK ABOUT AND DISCUSS

1. What is the difference between wisdom and knowledge? Who are the truly wise men and women of our generation? Suggest ways in which they have demonstrated their wisdom.
2. How can we increase in wisdom? (Ps. 51:6; 111:10; Eph. 1:17; James 1:5). How does the way in which we use our time show our wisdom (or the lack of it)?
3. What things do you think most prevent a person from gaining and using wisdom?

3 From sense to sensuality

(2:1-11)

In his previous area of investigation, the Preacher has searched for the meaning of life in wisdom. Disillusioned, he changes tack completely and embraces the world of pleasure, stepping from a narrow path to a much broader one.

I f, as we have supposed, the Preacher is writing from the perspective of Solomon, he is creating a great problem for himself, for he has already tasted the joy of God's kingdom. He is a child of the narrow way and will not find what he is looking for on the broad way. In effect, he turns from sense to sensuality and finds it senseless!

There is nothing intrinsically wrong with pleasure. The Bible speaks of the Christian life as being a pleasurable one (Ps. 16:11; 81:16; Exod. 23:25). The legitimate pleasures of this life, however, are a by-product of its first cause—to glorify God and enjoy him for ever. Jesus spoke of seeking the treasures of God's kingdom above everything else (Matt. 6:31-33).

However, the Bible warns us not to become ensnared even by the legitimate pleasure. The apostle Paul speaks of those who are 'lovers of pleasure rather than lovers of God' (2 Tim. 3:4). James warns those who seek God's blessing on their self-centred pursuit of pleasure (James 4:3). In his wholehearted attempt to find meaning and purpose in sensual pleasures, the Preacher abandons this overriding principle. To look for meaning and purpose in pleasure alone is to alienate ourselves from the God who has provided them for us. He has become like a child, whistling in the dark, seeking some diversion or comfort from a fear of the futility. He now reveals his areas of investigation.

He tries to lighten up (v. 1)

It is difficult to know what is in his mind as he approaches this point in his journey. The language he employs suggests that he is not simply launching himself into debauchery. This is a controlled experiment based on a legitimate philosophical system. But, however true this is, he is entering an area of human experience where self-control is difficult to maintain.

The hedonist schools of philosophy taught this approach to the meaning of life. The most well known and moderate form was Epicureanism. The apostle Paul encountered this when he addressed the Athenians on Mars Hill (Acts 17:18). Epicurus taught that through the avoidance of pain and the pursuit of pleasure people could attain happiness. These theories are prevalent in our own day when many would agree with the Preacher when he says, 'man has nothing better under the sun than to eat, drink, and be merry' (8:15). Modern life is based almost solely upon this aim. The problem is that if we embrace hedonism, it will soon embrace us and blind us to eternal truth.

The Preacher concludes that this is nothing but vanity. His words were echoed by Aldous Huxley when he wrote: 'Oh, how desperately bored, in spite of their grim determination to have a good time, the majority of pleasure seekers really are!'[1]

Laugh and the world laughs with you (v. 2)

Having abandoned his solemn pursuit for meaning and purpose, the Preacher introduces his first port of call in the sea of the senses. Laughter can have a therapeutic quality. In his book *Anatomy of an Illness,* Norman Cousins tells of how he overcame an incurable disease by enveloping himself in laughter. The world holds great store by laughter. A sense of humour can diffuse difficult situations and can bring light relief to many of the dire predicaments that man has found himself in. But such humour is often a cover for fear and despair. Ella Wheeler Wilcox's famous poem *Solitude* sums it up:

Laugh and the world laughs with you

Weep and you weep alone

For the sad old earth must borrow its mirth

But has trouble enough of its own![2]

Laughter can take a number of forms. It can be good and wholesome—when the humorous side of a situation is seen, or a good joke is told. It can even be an expression of great joy in the Lord (Deut. 28:47). However, laughter can also be derisive (Jer. 20:7; Mark 5:40). Abraham and Sarah's laughter expressed their incredulity at God's promise to them

(Gen. 17:17; 18:12). It can also be a cover-up for deep sorrow and disillusionment. Solomon himself warns us of this: 'Even in laughter the heart may sorrow, and the end of mirth may be grief'(Prov. 14:13). The comedian Tony Hancock brought laughter to millions through his radio and television shows. Yet he was a tortured genius—unsure of himself and frightened of his destiny. He tragically ended his own life in Australia in 1968. Stripped of his make-up, the clown is often a sad and pathetic figure. The life and soul of the party is often the loneliest person in the room.

The cup that cheers? (v. 3)

The Preacher's second port of call is the bar—or maybe just the vineyard! He is launching himself into a deep and thorough investigation of the pleasures of life—and he is doing it with his whole being! He is not simply drowning his sorrows in alcohol—

> Wine is the first person in the trinity of sensuous abandonment—wine, women and song!

people who do this are not investigating pleasure at all. He gives us a clue to the sphere in which he is moving by the words: 'while guiding my heart with wisdom', and, 'how to lay hold on folly'. Here are the two levels at which he is operating.

The first suggests that he is wholly embracing the good life. Wine is suggestive of many things attached to this— celebration, sophistication, wealth and epicureanism at its most sublime. Wine is the first person in the trinity of sensuous abandonment—wine, women and song! Of all the people of his day, Solomon is the most able to engage in this pursuit. He has his own vineyards and the capacity to import the finest wines.

The second phrase, 'how to lay hold on folly', suggests a less noble path in his pursuit. Many commentators have taken great pains to protect the Preacher's reputation by limiting his quest to epicureanism alone. Surely, however, a man who is so wholeheartedly throwing himself into the pleasures of the grape will at some point investigate its effect on the brain! He may not descend into drunken debauchery, but he will want to know whether the effect of alcohol will give him some kind of relief for the torment of a mind that cannot cope with the futility of its existence. Man has long pursued an altered state of consciousness through the use of alcohol and drugs.

The Preacher is aware of the folly of all this. He was once close to God, and the answer to the apparent meaninglessness of life is to be found in God alone. The apostle Paul echoed this when he wrote, 'And do not be drunk with wine, in which is dissipation, but be filled with the Spirit' (Eph. 5:18).

The last phrase of the verse forms a link with the more worthwhile pursuits he now engages in: 'till I might see what was good for the children of man to do under heaven all the days of their lives'. Alcohol has failed—it is now time to engage in something more worthwhile.

'If you want to see my monument, look around' (vv. 4-6)

The architect Christopher Wren was proud of his buildings. His greatest, St. Paul's Cathedral, prompted the words that head this section. On a lesser scale, most people see their homes as the main focus for their meaning and purpose in this world. They are our biggest investment of money and time. This is borne out by the numerous books, magazines and television programmes aimed at improving homes and gardens.

Solomon was able to do this on a grand scale. The motive for these projects can be seen by the emphasis he places on the word *myself*. Solomon was a great builder (1 Kings 7:1-8; 2 Chr. 8:3-6), yet there is no mention here of his greatest project, the Temple, in Jerusalem. The Song of Solomon refers to his vineyard at Baal Hamon (S. of S. 8:11). His houses were surrounded by great gardens (1 Kings 21:2).

Here are projects that most people can relate to—the creation of their own mini-environment. This may bring much satisfaction and lasting pleasure but can never truly satisfy. For so many people, these projects become the driving force of their existence. It is interesting to note the Preacher's use of the word *pardesim*—the Persian for 'a walled garden'—enjoyed only by the rich and privileged. Maybe he was trying to create his own form of paradise?

Power and prosperity (vv. 7-8)

Solomon could afford to possess anything material he chose. This even included fellow human beings! Power over people has always been a strong driving force within the human psyche. For some it becomes obsessive, and, indeed, the only means by which some people can achieve any sense of satisfaction or purpose. A powerful personality will also attract others. The pursuit of power as a goal or end, however, is insatiable and it inevitably corrupts those who have sought it for their chief end.

In 1991, facing financial difficulties, Robert Maxwell drowned while yachting off the Canary Islands. The exact circumstances of his death were unclear—a Spanish judge ruled out foul play, but did not determine how the death occurred. It was discovered that Maxwell had propped up his empire by diverting hundreds of millions of pounds from pension funds and other sources. It was a major financial fiasco, and Maxwell's empire was dissolved and sold off in the following years. Solomon's wealth exceeded anything men like Maxwell could have dreamed of.

'If music be the food of love…play on' (v. 8)

Music has always been a powerful expression of man's experience of life. From triumph to tragedy, from raw sexuality to deep spirituality, he has expressed himself through music. Soldiers have marched into battle with songs on their lips. Troubled minds, like that of King Saul, have been quieted by the sound of gentle music. Nations have their anthems—lovers have 'their tune'. Solomon, the son of a poet and musician, had even contributed his own lyrics to the Jewish hymnbook.

Music is also a powerful means in influencing people for good and for evil, from the glorious hymns of praise that have enriched the church over the centuries to the satanic lyrics and mind numbing percussion of 'heavy metal'. For some, it can become a consuming passion. In Dylan Thomas' *Under Milk Wood*, Mrs Organ Morgan says, 'Oh, I'm a martyr to music!' [3]

The phrase 'musical instruments of all kinds' is uncertain. The Hebrew can refer to a number of things—cupbearer, goblet, musical instrument, chest, and mistress, lover or concubine. The context of the Preacher's hedonistic pursuit of pleasure, coupled with what we know of Solomon, would more readily render it as 'many concubines' (ESV) or 'and a harem as well' (NIV).

'Fame! I'm gonna live for ever...' (v. 9)

> I'm gonna learn how to fly!
> High! I feel it coming together, people will see me and cry;
> Fame! I'm gonna make it to heaven, light up the sky like a flame;
> Fame! I'm gonna live for ever, remember my name.

Today, we live in the cult of the celebrity—some just seem to be famous for being famous. The anticipation of being recognized in the street is a heady drug for some people. Yet, for those who have experienced it, it can become a poisoned chalice. In a conversation recorded the day before her tragic death, Marilyn Monroe said, 'Fame will go by and, so long, I've had you, fame. If it goes by, I've always known that it was fickle. So at least it's something I experienced, but its not where I live.' Solomon was the most famous person of his day—even the Queen of Sheba paid court to him!

A reality check (vv. 9-10)

It seems at first that these pursuits are beginning to have the desired effect. The Preacher still appears to maintain his integrity (v. 9). He even begins to receive some satisfaction from his pursuits (v. 10). But he is brought crashing to the ground when he takes stock of his position (v. 11).

A desire to seek meaning and purpose for life in the gratification of the sense fails miserably. Not because the pursuits are meaningless in themselves—for God has given us a senuous nature and the ability to enjoy it to the full. But, like wisdom and, in the end, everything else we pursue,these things have no meaning when they are simply an end in themselves. Once again the 'under the sun' way of looking at life is found to be futile.

FOR FURTHER STUDY

1. The Preacher is a child of the narrow way. He turns from sense to sensuality and finds it senseless! Look up some biblical examples of this (1 Sam. 27-31; Luke 15:11-32), and note the Bible's warning (2 Tim. 3:1-9; James 4:1-6). What other examples can you think of?

2. Note the number of times the word 'I' occurs in this passage. Compare this with the attitude and teaching of Jesus (Phil. 2:5-11; Mark 8:34-38) and Paul (Gal. 2:20; Phil. 3:1-11).

TO THINK ABOUT AND DISCUSS

1. What are the things you most enjoy? How can you glorify God in them (1 Cor. 10:31)?

2. Can you identify a point where God-given pleasures can become sin (Luke 18:18-23)?

3. What guidelines might be applicable to Christians in engaging in what may be considered debatable practices such as drinking wine?

4 Acquisition and acquiescence

(2:17-26)

Unable to find satisfaction in wisdom or pleasure, the Preacher turns to the world of work, looking for 'job satisfaction'. He also reveals a shift in perspective—recognizing the overruling hand of God in everything.

The Preacher's pursuit naturally divides itself into two categories: *acquisition* and *acquiescence*. Before he introduces them, he emphasizes his current position (v.17). The word translated 'hated' speaks of weariness, antipathy and disgust, rather than a deep sense of hostility. He could have enjoyed life and all the things he had investigated, if only he had not asked that question, 'What does it all mean?' Having asked the question he is committed to its meaningless answer—thus his disgust with life!

Life on the treadmill (v. 17)

Why is he disgusted with life? Because of the apparent

pointless grind of it all. The French philosopher, E. M. Cioran, writes with the tragic and despairing air of someone with an under the sun mentality: 'Afflicted with existence, each man endures like an animal the consequences which proceed from it. Thus, in a world where everything is detestable, hatred becomes huger than the world and, having transcended its object, cancels itself out.' [1]

His hatred also is a product of his natural sinful heart—it has been aroused in him through his continual pursuit for the meaning of life without God. This reveals the ultimate folly of his position. He is caught on a treadmill—hating life, but afraid to die (v. 18). We see a marked contrast when we compare this with the Christian attitude, expressed by John Calvin when he said, 'Thou bruisest me, O Lord, but it amply sufficeth me that it is thy hand.'

The Preacher is encountering the same problem throughout his investigation. However promising each area is in fulfilling his desire for meaning and purpose, it is always brought to a futile and abrupt conclusion by death.

The area governed by this passage is no different, for he finds two contrasting features as he throws himself into his work.

Acquisition (vv. 18-23)

Acquisition is the act of gaining something through one's own efforts. The Preacher has worked long and hard in gaining many things over the course of his life. He now recognizes the futility of it all. His successor will inherit his estate without any concept of the time and energy expended in its acquirement.

Work can become a consuming thing. It takes up our time, our energy and our interest. For some, it may be motivated by a desire to contribute to the well-being of others—but there are those who believe it to be the only means by which they can gain position and respect. Whatever our non-materialistic motives for work, it is a stark fact of life that we all have to earn a living. The difficulty is when to say, 'Enough', and turn our attention to more important things—our worship and service for God, our families and friends and recreation.

A totalitarian demand (vv. 18-22)

It is difficult to do this in a society that is geared to material and social achievement. We are urged to acquire more and our acquisitive nature often shouts a loud 'Amen'. Jesus warned of this when he said, 'You cannot serve God and mammon' (Matt. 6:24). It is interesting to observe how he gives materialism a god-like status! Martyn Lloyd-Jones speaks of the 'totalitarian demand' that these things make upon us. He goes on to say: 'How they tend to grip the whole personality and affect us everywhere! They demand our entire devotion; they want us to live for them absolutely.'[2] This powerful view of the dangers of materialism is not exclusive to evangelical Christians. Greed is the natural consequence of materialism. The humanistic psychotherapist, Erich Fromm, describes it as, 'a bottomless pit which exhausts the person in endless effort to satisfy the need without ever reaching satisfaction.'[3] Someone has

> We are urged to acquire more and our acquisitive nature often shouts a loud 'Amen'.

likened the pursuit of the world's riches to gathering nuts. Clothes are torn in getting them, teeth are broken in chewing them, and the stomach is never filled in eating them.

This is the plight of all who are in the grip of materialism. Sadly, there are Christians who have become so embroiled in their work—for materialistic or other reasons—that they have lost their sense of priority and pine for the joy they once knew. In pursuing this avenue of meaning and purpose, the Preacher has found this to be true. He describes his work as 'burdensome' and 'striving of his heart'.

In the light of this, what can be gained by acquisition? Even if we were able to say, 'Enough', what would we gain in the end? As always, Jesus hits the nail firmly on the head in the parable of the rich fool (Luke 12:16-21). Here is a man who seems more than satisfied with his labours—even echoing the Preacher's words: 'eat, drink and be merry'—yet his self-satisfaction is merely a tragic illusion because God will require his soul that very night! 'Then,' says Jesus, 'whose will those things be which you have provided?' (Luke 12:20).

This leads us on to the Preacher's next conclusion.

You can't take it with you (vv. 21-23)

What will happen to your work and wealth when you leave it behind? After Solomon's death his son, Rehoboam, inherited all that the king had laboured for. But he did not have his father's wisdom, so the power and wealth were soon dissipated. On a smaller scale, we see this repeated time and time again. When I was a boy we often went to a local shop that never seemed to close. It was open early in the morning until as late as possible in the evening, seven days a week! The only time the proprietor was seen outside his shop was at the crack of dawn, when he took his dog for a walk. On rare occasions, he was joined at the counter by his wife, who made it clear to everyone within earshot that she had other interests. The shop was there throughout my childhood and into my early twenties. One day, the man collapsed and died while serving a customer. His wife took over the shop and announced that she was selling up, and was going to spend the money doing all the things he had denied her over the years. She even showed me the brochure of the world-cruise she had booked!

Are there not countless stories of widows, sons and daughters inheriting businesses that have lovingly and sacrificially been built up by a man's labours, only to bring the whole edifice down with a short period of time through incompetence, irresponsibility, lack of interest, or simply having different priorities. What is the greatest legacy we can leave others—a business, a large sum of money, an education—with all the sacrifices these may entail? The answer must be a resounding, 'No!' And, if you have no one to succeed you, what is the point of acquisition anyway?

Acquiescence (vv. 24-26)

These verses indicate a turning point in the Preacher's despairing, nihilistic outlook. Although his final conclusion will be the same, he introduces two striking admissions that show that his original cynicism about life having no meaning and purpose is flawed. Firstly, he glances above the sun. God, who is alluded to in chapter 1:13, now becomes a factor in the equation. Secondly, he admits that it is possible to find enjoyment under the sun. The introduction of the first enables the second. We can see this clearly when we look at the passage in greater detail.

A new perspective (vv. 24-25)

In the previous section he is concerned with acquisition—a life bent on gathering to itself every possible joy attainable on this earth—in this particular instance, the joy obtained from the fruits of a man's labour. Having abandoned this as futile, he now takes the opposite position and simply acquiesces to the will of God. Here is a hopeful note in the gloom.

We see a number of contrasts with what he has said before. The problem is not with the things, but with the thinking. He has now conceded that what he had previously found meaningless was 'from the hand of God' (v. 24), and he begins to view things in a different light. Although he is still far from being out of the gloom, he reveals that there are shafts of light appearing. When the blessings of this life are seen as the products of our own labour, they are fragile. When we see them as being from the hand of God, they take on a new dimension. They are stripped of their vulnerability and we do not become afraid of losing them. In fact, the very act of acquiescing to the will of God, and rejoicing in what he has

> When the blessings of this life are seen as the products of our own labour, they are fragile. When we see them as being from the hand of God, they take on a new dimension.

chosen to bestow upon us, enables us to enjoy the material blessings in a way that we have never done before. As the hymn writer puts it:

> Heaven above is softer blue,
> Earth around is sweeter green;
> Something lives in every hue,
> Christless eyes have never seen;
> Birds with gladder songs o'erflow,
> Flowers with deeper beauties shine,
> Since I know, as now I know,
> I am his, and he is mine.

We see the shift in the Preacher's thinking by the way in which he speaks of wisdom and knowledge. Previously he has referred to them as something acquired—'I have attained... and have gained' (1:16). Now he acknowledges that they are a gift from God (v. 26). In doing so he highlights the difference between the two perspectives. Previously, wisdom has brought him much grief, and knowledge has only added to his sorrow. Now he takes the opposite view— to wisdom and knowledge he now adds joy!

A new position (v. 26)

There are two factors that make up the Preacher's new position. Firstly, he sees the overruling hand of God in everything. He is aware of God's sovereignty in giving joy alongside the material benefits he bestows upon men. Secondly, he recognizes the gulf between the man who is good and the man who is sinful.

A number of commentators have pointed out that he is not referring specifically to the saved or the unsaved. It is primarily a matter of perspective. This is brought home in the conclusion of the chapter: 'This also is vanity and grasping for the wind'. It is difficult to know exactly what he means by this. Is he simply referring to God's sovereignty in the matter, or is he writing about those who are simply good or bad in their attitude to such blessing? There are those who view life with a total 'under the sun' dimension—while others glance above the temporal and see the hand of a Creator at work in the world. In doing so, do they please God and enjoy his blessing in the process? Whatever the Preacher means, an overall biblical perspective shows us that the only sure and certain way to please God, and truly enjoy his blessings, is to enter into a living relationship with him! 'Without faith it is impossible to please him, for he who comes to God must believe that he is, and that he is a rewarder of those who diligently seek him' (Heb. 11:6).

The blessings that are common to all men take on a new dimension as they are sealed with covenant love. This is exemplified by Paul's exhortation: 'Therefore, whether you eat or drink, or whatever you do, do all to the glory of God' (1 Cor. 10:31). The sinner knows nothing of this. His life is an endless round of acquisition, without ever truly gaining from his labour. In fact, the Preacher shows that even his labours are directed to the good of the godly (v. 26).

If our lives are in the spirit of acquiescence to God, we gain everything we need in this world—and more! (Eph. 3:20). Herein lies one of the great biblical principles for happiness.

FOR FURTHER STUDY

1. The Preacher is the 'man who has everything'. Read though the passage and pick out the negative words he uses to describe his response to life. Why does he hate life so much?

2. How do verses 24-26 indicate a shift in the Preacher's thinking? What do you think prompted that shift (cf. 1 Kings 3:1-15; 11:1-13) ?

TO THINK ABOUT AND DISCUSS

1. Is it our circumstances or our attitude that determines our acquiescence to God's work in our lives (cf. Phil. 4:10-13)?

2. Can you identify with the Preacher's disillusionment in any area of your life? What positive steps can you take to rectify the matter?

3. Suggest as many examples as you are able to of people who have become disillusioned in life. How did their disillusionment show?

5 A poem with a purpose

(3:1-22)

In the midst of his search, the Preacher pauses for reflection. God is mentioned eight times in this chapter. This indicates that he is beginning to look above the sun for meaning and purpose.

Everything has a time (vv. 1-8)

The Hebrew in verse 1 refers to a specific moment rather than a period of time—denoting a predetermined purpose on which all things depend. Each human life has a span, and within its duration there are momentous events. Man may see them as random happenings—determined by the roll of the celestial dice—but the Bible teaches that God has a chosen purpose for everything (Rom. 8:28). Man has mastered many things, but he has no control over time. Each moment is God-appointed.

This poem contains fourteen opposites denoting completion—a common factor in Hebrew poetry.

Life and death (vv. 2-3)

The issue is both passive and active—birth and death are two ends of the spectrum of life. Man has no control over either—yet he is involved in the creation of new life through the process of conception and birth. He can stretch out the expanse of time through better health care, but he cannot halt its advance. It is clear that these issues weigh heavily upon the Preacher. Man is active in sowing and reaping, but he is not in control of the process of nature that determines the seasons and duration in which he must operate.

The act of killing is an inevitable part of life under the sun. Human life was taken in war and in the execution of justice; animals were sacrificed in the Temple rituals. Sin brought death into the world and, inevitably, man would become involved in its process. God, himself, ordered the killing of Israel's enemies and the sacrifices that would point to the perfect sacrifice of his own moment, when he gave up the life of his own Son.

Although the Preacher is drawing contrasts here, it is worth noting that killing and healing, breaking down and building-up, often go hand in hand as part of the same process. Certain bacteria and micro-organisms have to be killed before organs and tissue can be restored to health. As a builder, Solomon would have been well aware of the necessity to tear down a dangerous and dilapidated building before rebuilding on the same site. There is a time for both kinds of action in the process of healing and construction. The Christian life is full of such metaphors. For example, the apostle Paul tells us to put to death the misdeeds of the body

(Rom. 8:13; Col. 3:5), in order to put on the new life we have in Christ (Col. 3:10). We are to reckon ourselves as being dead to sin and alive to God (Rom. 6:11) Jesus even depicted his own death in the same way: 'Destroy this temple, and in three days I will raise it up' (John 2:19-22).

The second couplet deals with the deep emotion that we experience as we pass through life under the sun (v. 4). The Preacher speaks here of inner feeling and its outward expression. We will all face times of rejection or bereavement when we will be plunged into mourning. Conversely, there will be times of joy—maybe so unbridled that we will even dance! The Bible speaks of the victory of joy over mourning for those who have drawn close to God through Jesus Christ (Ps. 30:5; 3:6-8; Rev. 7:17; 21:4).

Friendship and enmity (v. 5)

This particular section has been prone to a number of interpretations. Some interpretations of the stones metaphor include: the old Jewish practice of dropping stones into an open grave, the preparation for the building of a house, the building of a memorial, and the destruction of the temple and God's judgement. A simple interpretation could be found in the practice of ancient armies in covering an enemy's field with stones in order to make it unproductive (2 Kings 3:19,25), and the removal of stones from a field before planting (Isa. 5:2). Gordon Keddie suggests the additional picture of the preparation of the highway for the advance of the victorious army (Isa. 62:10).[1] The overall message, however, is that in human experience there are times of friendship and there are times of enmity.

Receiving and giving (v. 6)

There is a kind of activity and passivity in his understanding of their role. Man is active in the gaining and giving away, but passive in the losing and keeping. This reveals the interchange of circumstances that we all experience as we go through life. Some things are within our control—others are outside of it. A person may build up a business and lose it through collapse of the financial market. A loved one may be taken from us in a tragic accident. On the other hand, there are times when we must voluntarily part with things that we may hold dear to us. The whole idea in the Preacher's mind is to put possession into context: gain, but be prepared to lose; keep, but be prepared to give away. As John Wesley advised his followers, 'Gain all you can; save all you can; give all you can.'

> The whole idea in the Preacher's mind is to put possession into context: gain, but be prepared to lose; keep, but be prepared to give away.

Destruction and creativity (v. 7)

Many commentators take the view that this verse refers to the mourning process. The tearing and silence depicting a time of grief and the sewing and speaking the recovery. This is the natural expression of grief in the Old Testament. David and his men tear their clothes in mourning for Saul and Jonathan (2 Sam. 1:11), and Job did likewise as he heard of the loss of his children (Job 1:20). The Bible also depicts it as a sign of anger or exasperation (Matt. 26:65; Acts 14:14;

16:22). Whether both parts of this verse follow the same theme is debatable. It may simply mean the wisdom of knowing the proper place to speak and refrain from speaking. The New Testament emphasizes this. James speaks of the taming of the tongue (James 3:3-12), and Paul the need for grace in our speech (Col. 4:6). Jesus epitomizes the wisdom theme as he stands before Pontius Pilate (Matt. 27:11-14).

Love and hate (v. 8)

It is important to note that the Preacher is not advocating or approving these things, but simply recording them as being grounded in human experience. The experience of war and peace is grounded in the emotions of love and hate. This principle is taken up by and perfected by Jesus in the Sermon on the Mount where murder and adultery begin in the heart before manifesting themselves in action.

Everything has a purpose (vv. 9-15)

God's purpose is seen in the interweaving of time with eternity where labours are 'God-given tasks'(v. 10). In 'under the sun' thinking, we are still in the realm of meaninglessness. But in the life of the Christian, these labours have a purpose. We see this clearly depicted by the apostle Peter when he speaks of the testing of our faith (1 Peter 1:6-9)

The purpose of beauty (v. 11)

It would be easy to interpret this in the same vein as Andy Warhol's famous phrase, 'Everyone will be famous for fifteen minutes!' It may well be true that, as the song says, 'Everything is beautiful in its own way', but this is not the point that the Preacher is conveying here. The Hebrew gives the picture of a set or appointed time. The beauty comes in recognizing and acknowledging the place and purpose of every person, thing, or event in God's overall plan. This is all we can do, for the second part of the verse tells us that even though God has given us the ability to investigate and try to make sense of his handiwork, we cannot fathom the mystery of divine providence unless God chooses to reveal it to us. As Michael Eaton says, 'God's disposal of events in their "times" is beautiful'.[2]

The purpose of satisfaction (vv. 12-13)

There is an air of cynicism bordering on futility about the Preacher's use of the term, 'nothing better'. His concept is redeemed by the regulating factor, 'it is the gift of God.' In 'under the sun' thinking, all the previous factors have a sense of futility about them—recognition that the delights and services of our earthly lives are God-given takes them into a dimension of satisfaction.

The purpose of eternity (v. 14)

Without God, everything suffers in the futility of temporality. The pleasures and even the good works of this life are simply a means of marking time until its inevitable cessation, when everything will be snatched from our grasp. The Preacher highlights the permanence, completeness and security that are to be found

> Without God, everything suffers in the futility of temporality.

in the realization that God has an eternal purpose in all that he does. This purpose is to engender fear into the heart of man! This fear may initially bring thoughts of dread and terror to the heart of man, but its intent is to give recognition of God's awesome power and authority.

The purpose of lasting service (v. 15)

Unlike life 'under the sun' the believer experiences the enduring nature of God's kingdom. This verse gives perspective to the cyclical, unchangeable events of man's life and history. The treadmill of life and death that he previously described as 'vanity' has now, with the recognition of God's sovereignty, become a secure environment in which he can gladly experience the hand of God at work.

Everything has a destiny (vv. 16-22)

The previous section concluded that 'God requires an account of what is past'. The Preacher now goes on to show us the nature of this accounting from two perspectives.

God's perspective (vv. 16-17)

We begin in the place where man is called to exercise a God-like function—justice. In the courts of law, where true judgment was called to prevail, there was wickedness. This was rooted in the nature of fallen man. True justice could not prevail because true judgement cannot be made without righteousness. In its place there was iniquity. We are called to make judgements throughout our lives as to another person's character, abilities, actions, but these judgements will always be impaired in some way by our sin. Only God is the righteous judge, and the Preacher shows us that God is testing man so he can see clearly that in this area he is, in effect, little more than an animal. He, too, will face the true righteous Judge. Man's destiny is to face the judgement of God.

Man's perspective (vv. 18-22)

The Preacher goes on to show us that fallen man sees things from a different angle. He sees the same things, but views them in a different way. In acknowledging the failures of his own race in exercising justice and acting in righteousness, he concludes that he is no more than an animal of a different species. His destiny is no different from a dog or any other living creature. It is easy to see that, once this philosophy is adopted, man will perceive his origin to be the same.

> What fallen man needs is revelation: someone to show him the true reality of his position in the mind and heart of God; someone to show him his destiny.

Is there any hope in this scenario? The Preacher concludes with a provocative question, 'For who can bring him to see what will happen after him?' What fallen man needs is revelation: someone to show him the true reality of his position in the mind and heart of God; someone to show him his destiny. In asking the question, the Preacher leaves it open to us to pursue the answer, which is to be found clearly within the pages of the Bible.

For further study ▶

FOR FURTHER STUDY

1. Notice how the principle of God's 'appointed time' figured in the life of Jesus (Gal. 4:4; John 7:1-9; 7:25-31; 1 Cor. 4:5).

2. What are the negatives and positives of verses 9-15?

3. What do the following passages tell us about the nature of God's judgement: Ps. 82:1-5; Acts 17:29-31; Luke 18:7-8; Rev. 6:9-11?

TO THINK ABOUT AND DISCUSS

1. How does God's timing apply to our salvation (Ps. 31:15; Mark 1:15; Rom. 5:6)?

2. If God is sovereign, how are we to view the injustices of life (vv. 16-22)?

3. What would you say to a colleague at work, a friend at university or a family member who challenges you about your belief in the essential goodness of God?

6 The crying game

(4:1-16)

The Preacher takes an honest look at life under the sun, and sees the tears of a mankind that has lost its way. He looks and sees that a life lived on earth without God ultimately brings exploitation, frustration, loneliness and disillusionment. Amid the laughter and gaiety is a vale of tears.

For so many people, life is, seemingly, nothing more than a lottery. We all appear to be victims of chance—all subject to the way the wind blows. The Chinese materialist philosopher, Fan Chen, wrote, 'Human life may be likened to the leaves on yonder tree. The wind blows down the flowers, of which some are the screens and scattered on the beautifully decorated mats and cushions, while others are blown over the fence and dropped on the dung heap.'

Through the course of a human life many tears are shed. The Preacher focuses on some of the causes.

The tears of the oppressed (vv. 1-3)

These seem to be the words of a helpless bystander observing the exploitation of the weak by the powerful. Yet Solomon is a man who is in a position to do something about oppression and exploitation within his own kingdom but, as he turns to other gods, he abandons the sacred trust that God has given him as king of Israel (1 Kings 11). Yet God has declared his desire for justice for the exploited: '"For the oppression of the poor, for the sighing of the needy, now I will arise", says the Lord; "I will set him in the safety for which he yearns", (*cf.* Ps. 12:5). Wherever there is power there is the temptation for its misuse. This can operate on a national scale, as in the case of rulers (Prov. 28:16); at a local level (Eccles. 5:8; Jer. 7:6)); and even in the church (1 Peter 5:1-3)!

Some of us have visited and worked in countries ruled by oppressive regimes and have encountered the chain of exploitation and oppression as it has filtered down through the army, police and petty bureaucrats, and on to the streets of the cities, towns and villages. For many, in the Third World, this seems to be their only way to survival. In such circumstances the Christian citizen is faced with a dilemma. Not only is he exploited, and in many cases oppressed because of his faith, he will often find himself in a position where he, too, is tempted to become part of the system.

For those of us living in a democracy, exploitation becomes more subtle and personal—but just as hurtful. Children encounter bullying at school and some are even driven to suicide! Such behaviour does not end with our childhood; it simply becomes subtler as it enters the workplace and even the home. Inevitably we see another kind of chain in operation—the bullied can look for someone weaker to bully—the abused becomes the abuser. Satan, the arch-exploiter, takes man's fallen human nature and distorts the image of a God of justice in whose likeness we are created. The poignant cry of the Preacher is repeated, 'they have no comforter'—and it comes from the heart of a man who is aware of his own exploitative nature.

The Preacher sees no way out other than death. Notice the despairing cynicism in verses 2 and 3. 'Caught up in this web of exploitation,' he is saying, 'it is better that I had never been born.' A slogan in the Spanish Civil War declared: 'Long live death! Down with intelligence!' The Preacher, the most intelligent of men, can find no comfort in this world of exploitation—for him, death seems to be the better option.

The tears of the frustrated (vv. 4-6)

Ernest Lehman called it 'The Sweet Smell of Success'. Millions labour for its fragrance in one field or another—but at what price? Underlying its pursuit and gain is a trait of fallen human nature that ultimately frustrates both the successful and those around them. This is one of the Preacher's tragic findings as he delves into the meaning and purpose of life under the sun. Envy can be both the motivation for success and the result of success.

> The Preacher, the most intelligent of men, can find no comfort in this world of exploitation—for him, death seems to be the better option.

Our ambitions may appear to have their roots in altruistic soil, but they can easily be fed and watered by our envy of others. People speak of 'healthy competition', but Solomon saw that much of this was the result of envy and nothing more than 'rottenness to the bones' (Prov. 14:30). The Bible gives us many instances of the insatiability of envy—of those who have much that crave for more. Ahab had a kingdom, but killed a man for a vineyard (1 Kings 21); Solomon's father had many wives and concubines, yet stole another man's wife (2 Sam. 11).

Envy of the success of others can often ruin relationships. Gore Vidal was brutally frank when he said, 'Whenever a friend succeeds, a little something in me dies.' How often have we wished someone success but secretly wanted him or her to fail? Achievement under the sun, that does not put God first, will leave you frustrated, because its motivating force is envy—and envy will never be satisfied.

What makes it more frustrating is found in what follows in verse 5. Here is a dramatic contrast to the verse that precedes it and a springboard to the verse that follows. The folding of the hands was a traditional saying describing, what we would call today, the 'drop-out'. In his collection of Proverbs, Solomon uses the term to highlight the foolishness of indolence (Prov. 6:10; 24:33). Here he graphically portrays such a condition as self-cannibalism!

The Preacher now throws in a balancing factor (v. 6). Here is the middle way between excessive acquisition and indolence but, because of the power of envy, the balance is virtually impossible to achieve. Man's fallen nature craves 'just a little more'. Pythagorus invented an ingenious cup that could be filled with water to a line about an inch below the brim. Any attempt to add more water resulted in the loss of the lot through a hole in the bottom! I tried it—and had wet trousers to prove it!

The tears of the lonely (vv. 7-12)

The Preacher now puts himself in the shoes of a lonely man. What is the root cause of this man's loneliness? He has no immediate family. Maybe he is an only child who has lost both his parents? Why has he never married? The context suggests that he is describing someone who is so consumed by his work, he is incapable of making or keeping close relationships. There are those who have achieved things in life, who have lost their families and friendships along the way. If such a person asks the question, 'For whom do I toil?' the answer only reinforces their sense of loneliness. Former Secretary-General of the United Nations, Dag Hammarskjöld, once wrote, 'What makes loneliness an anguish is not that I have no one to share my burden, but this: I have only my own burden to bear.' [1]

Success is meaningless when it becomes all consuming. Think of the politician or businessman who rises to the top of his profession, only to realize that he has lost his family in the process, or a person consumed by his hobbies to the extent where the family is pushed out. For most, the question, 'For whom do I toil?' comes too late!

The Preacher highlights the effects of such loneliness by contrasting them with the joys of togetherness (v. 9). In many cases two people can enjoy more than double success for their labours. There are some instances where a man cannot work alone, for he needs 'another pair of hands'. An ancient Jewish proverb says, 'A friendless man is like the left hand bereft of the right.' Success is something to be shared. At moments of triumph we instinctively turn to another in the shared moment. As two are better than one in triumph— then this holds good for times of difficulty and even tragedy (v. 10). The Bible instructs us to 'Bear one another's burdens (Gal. 6:2). George Eliot described a best friend as 'a well-spring in the wilderness.'

The Preacher goes on to speak of the warmth of human relationships. His picture is very practical (v. 11). This can obviously be seen as a reference to marriage, but it must be noted that travellers often slept together on cold nights. Towards the end of his life, Solomon's father, David, slept with the virgin Abishag simply for the warmth of her body.

The final verse of this section focuses upon protection (v. 12). For travellers, in the time of the Preacher, it was advisable to have a companion. Lone travellers were easy prey to robbers. Jesus aptly illustrates this in the parable of the Good Samaritan (Luke 10:25-37). The mention of the 'threefold cord' reminds us of the strength of fellowship. If one companion is advisable, how much better to have two. The two travellers on the road to Emmaus were joined by a third (Luke 24:15).

The tears of the disillusioned (vv. 13-16)

The Preacher now tells us a 'rags to riches story'. There have been many attempts to identify the historical characters behind the story. Some have suggested Joseph and Pharaoh, Saul and David, Astyages and Cyrus, and others. The story, however, simply typifies a principle that has been duplicated a million times in human history. Success—advancement—power—popularity—are all fleeting. Those who look for permanent status will be disillusioned.

The old leader who once rose to prominence but has now become out of touch, 'past his sell-by date', supplanted by a younger, more dynamic, modern man who captures the imagination of the people, but who, in turn will go the way of the older leader and be supplanted by another. We see this repeated endlessly in every area of society in the lives of politicians, business executives, football managers etc. The tabloid newspapers build up someone into superstar status, only to bring him crashing down with a scandal either real or imaginary! Shakespeare's comment, 'Uneasy lies the head that bears the crown,' was true.

Conclusion

This passage began with the words, 'I returned and considered'. If we compare this with the words found in Revelation 7:9, 'I looked and behold', we see a different picture. John saw a great multitude praising God. The passage ends with the words, 'For the lamb who is in the midst of the throne will shepherd them and lead them to living fountains of waters. And God will wipe away every tear from their eyes' (Rev. 7:17).

For further study ▶

FOR FURTHER STUDY

1. What is God's attitude to the oppressed (v. 1 cf. Isa. 10:1-3; Hab. 2:6-14; James 5:1-6)?

2. What effect does materialism have upon a person (vv. 4-8)?

3. Has God forgotten us in the midst of oppression, frustration, loneliness and disillusionment (2 Kings 20:5; Ps. 30:5; Luke 7:11-17; John 20:11-18; Rev. 7:17)?

TO THINK ABOUT AND DISCUSS

1. Are you conscious of any of the negative effects of materialism in your life? If so, what steps could you take in order to rectify this?

2. Are you conscious of your need for companionship and help (vv. 9-12. cf. Acts 2:1, 44-47; 4:32-34)?

3. How valuable and lasting is popularity (vv. 13-16)? In what ways do you think Christians who become famous or popular can use their influence for the furtherance of the message of the gospel? Are there negative side effects that might need to be avoided?

7 Standing in awe of God

(5:1-7)

In previous chapters, the Preacher has shared his conclusions on the meaninglessness of life 'under the sun'. He now turns his attention to worship, an 'above the sun' activity, and warns his readers of the dangers of making even that meaningless.

In his book *That's Life*, Derek Tidball tells the story of a dinner guest at a Cambridge College who was asked to say grace before the meal. To make matters worse, it was to be said in Latin! Knowing neither God nor Latin, the quick-thinking fellow intoned, 'Omo, lux, domestos, brobat, ajax, Amen.' After repeating the 'Amen', everyone sat down to eat. No one had noticed! [1]

For many, worship can become a meaninglessness exercise. The Preacher takes great pains to make sure that it isn't.

Preparation for worship (v. 1)

How many of us take time to prepare for worship? Sunday morning can be the most hectic and fraught time of the week. The family needs to get ready for church, preparations must be made for visitors, elderly people may need lifts to the morning service. For the preacher and leaders there are numerous things to attend to before worship begins. It is almost with a sigh of relief that all the people take their places and begin the worship service. The Preacher gives two principles that prepare us inwardly for worship, however frenetic the outward preparations may have been.

The holiness of God

Firstly, we need to recognize the holiness of God. To 'walk prudently' is inwardly to obey the command given to Moses, 'Take your sandals off your feet, for the place where you stand is holy ground' (Exod. 3:5). In many parts of the world, the Christian preacher is required to remove his shoes before he enters the pulpit. The worship of Israel was centred upon this concept. The rites and rituals of Tabernacle and Temple worship were geared to proclaim and preserve this in the life of the people of Israel. The day of worship (Exod. 16:23; 20:8,11), the place (Exod. 26:33-34), the offering (Lev. 6:25-27), the priests (Lev. 21:7) and the worshippers (2 Chr. 20:21) were all to be holy before the Lord.

This, however, is not just an Old Testament theme. Jesus drove the money changers from the Temple courts (Matt. 21:12-17). Paul commands Christians to examine themselves before coming to the table of the Lord, lest they eat the bread and drink the cup 'in an unworthy manner' (1 Cor. 11:27-28). The reverence and godly fear of Old Testament worship is reinforced in New Testament teaching (Heb. 12:28-29). And, of course, overriding all of this is the command: 'You shall be holy, for I the LORD your God am holy' (Lev. 19:2).

Holiness has three dimensions. It begins with *reverence* towards the one whom we worship—recognizing and acknowledging his awesomeness and purity. It also means *to be set apart for God*. The Christian is one who has been set apart for salvation and becomes the instrument through whom

> How can we worship God aright if we do not make adequate preparation of heart and life?

God is worshipped and honoured. In order to do this, the worshipper and his worship is to be pure and sinless. How can we worship God aright if we do not make adequate preparation of heart and life?

The authority of God

Secondly, we are required to acknowledge the authority of God. We are commanded to 'draw near to hear'. When Jesus explained the nature of true worship to the Samaritan woman, he revealed that it must be 'in spirit and truth' (John 4:24). How can we worship in truth if we do not 'draw near to hear'? We cannot separate true worship from the proclamation of God's Word. 'The 'sacrifice of fools' is ignorant worship or worship in the flesh. It is well intended, but is unacceptable to God because it cannot be rooted in obedience if God's voice is not heard. Drawing near to hear denotes active listening for the voice of God as his Word is proclaimed or, as Thomas Watson put it, 'Many come to the Word only to feast their ears; they like the melody of the voice, the mellifluous sweetness of the expression, the newness of the notion (Acts 17:21). This is to love the garnishing of the dish more than the food; this is to desire to be pleased rather than edified. Like a woman that paints her face, but neglects her health.' [2]

If God's Word is faithfully expounded, then he will be speaking to his people. Sadly, too much emphasis is placed on the way the message is produced and delivered. How many conversations take place at the Sunday lunch table that pass judgement on the service? The hymns, prayers and especially the preaching become a topic of criticism based on whether or not they pleased the hearer. Such conversations should have taken place at the breakfast table where judgement should have begun at the readiness of the congregation to go to the place of worship and 'Walk prudently... and draw near to hear'! When we come to worship we should be prepared!

Presentation of worship (vv. 2-3)

A command

This section begins with a command to bridle the tongue. The pagan religions were noted for their lengthy incantations and mantras. These may well have crept into the worship of the living God—for Jesus warned his own generation, 'But when you pray, do not use vain repetitions as the heathen do. For they think that they will be heard for their many words.

Therefore do not be like them. For your Father knows the things you have need of before you ask him' (Matt. 6:7-8). The U.S. President, Calvin Coolidge, was noted for his reluctance in using more words than absolutely necessary. At a dinner party he was seated next to a well-known actress who informed him that she had bet someone that she could make him say at least three words during the evening. 'You lose,' replied Coolidge and remained silent for the rest of the meal.

It is not just the number of words that is at issue here. The Preacher warns of rashness and haste in speaking to God—a kind of thoughtless utterance of religious sentiment that has no true thought or purpose behind it. This is not just true for those who simply repeat a written liturgical formula each time they engage in corporate worship. The same can be said for the unwritten repetition that can easily become the norm in freer forms of worship. Actions and phrases that may well sincerely and thoughtfully stem from the heart of an individual worshipper can be picked up and duplicated by others who are impressed by its overt spirituality, yet have no concept of the true intent behind it.

The Preacher warns of rashness and haste in speaking to God—a kind of thoughtless utterance of religious sentiment that has no true thought or purpose behind it.

A reason (v. 2)

The Preacher proceeds to give a reason for such a command.

It is to be found in the distance between people and God. If we truly understood the gulf between a holy, enthroned God and a defiled, self-centred sinner, we would be rendered speechless. The act of worship is firstly a gracious action of God in bridging the gulf between himself and the worshipper through the merits of his Son, Jesus Christ the Great High Priest (Heb. 7:20 - 8:6). The presence of such a priest in the midst of God's people must surely elicit a deep sense of awe! John, 'in the Spirit on the Lord's Day', had a vision of the presence of Christ. The effect was electric! After describing what he saw and heard he can only recount, 'I fell at his feet as dead' (Rev. 1:17).

A picture (v. 3)

The Preacher draws a picture of the folly by comparing it with the produce of an over-busy mind. As Otto Zockler says, as an 'exciting and anxious occupation of the mind produces the phenomenon of confused and uneasy dreams by which the sleep is disturbed, soon the habit of an excess of words, causes the speech to degenerate into vain and senseless twaddle.' [3] The unconscious mind often makes a bizarre interpretation of the things that have occupied it during a busy day—relating current events with distant memories and often producing a scenario that would not seem out of place in a science fiction movie.

As Derek Kidner comments, 'The reiterated word *fool(s)* is scathing, for to be casual with God is an evil (1), a sin (6) and a provocation that will not go unpunished (6b).' [4]

Promises at worship (vv. 4-7)

The same sentiments are recorded by Solomon in his collection of proverbs: 'It is a snare for a man to devote rashly something as holy, and afterward to reconsider his vows' (Prov. 20:25).

The place of promises

Vows or promises were an integral part of Jewish worship. Worshippers committed themselves to some kind of action, usually the offering of sacrifices, if God would grant their requests (Gen. 28:20-22; 1 Sam. 1:11; Ps. 132:2-5). God's promises to his people are rehearsed time and time again as we meet with him in worship. It is fitting that we are not casual in the promises we might make to him. How sincere are we when we sing, 'O Jesus, I have promised to serve thee to the end?' for, as Matthew Henry points out, 'A vow is a bond upon the soul.' [5]

The responsibility of promises

Promises inevitably spring from an encounter with God in worship and Word. But, we must be careful, for the Preacher goes on to say, 'Better not to vow than to vow and not pay' (v. 5). It would appear that he is telling his readers that many vows made to God are unnecessary, but once made, must be kept. We see this tragically depicted in the story of Jephthah and his daughter (Judg. 11:29-40). How many idle promises do we make to God in the heat of the moment or in the charged atmosphere of a particular circumstance? How many have we fulfilled? Jesus taught that it was better to say nothing and then do the will of God than to make an idle promise that would remain unfulfilled (Matt. 21:28-31). Peter was quick to say to Jesus: 'Even if I have to die with you, I will not deny you!' (Matt. 26:35); yet it was not long before his words were rendered meaningless (Matt. 26:69-75).

The fulfilment of promises (v. 6)

The Preacher repeats the warning of verse 2, and then introduces another dimension—the messenger of God. The identity of the messenger is not revealed in the passage. Although the Hebrew can also be rendered as 'angel', it is likely that the Preacher is referring to a Temple messenger who collected unfulfilled vows on behalf of the priest. Simply to fob him off with, 'I'm sorry, it was all a mistake', will not work—the vow has not been made to him but to God! The New Testament tells the tragic story of Ananias and Sapphira who—during a time when many of the early Christians were selling property and giving the proceeds to God's work—sold a possession but only gave part of the proceeds to the apostles, thus deceiving them into believing that they had acted with integrity and generosity. God, however, could not be deceived—with tragic consequences (Acts 5:1-11). Such passages show us the awesome responsibility we have to be slow in making promises to God that we cannot keep or withholding from God that which is rightfully his!

The Preacher sums it up thus: 'For in the multitude of dreams and many words there is also vanity. But fear God' (5:7).

A summary

Prepare for worship—present your worship in a God-ordered way—promises must be seriously considered—above all, stand in awe of God!

FOR FURTHER STUDY

1. Note the elements of holiness found in both Old and New Testament worship (Exod. 16:23; 20:8-11; 26:33-34; Lev. 6:25-27; 21:7; 2 Chr. 20:21; 1 Cor. 11:27-34; Heb. 12:25-29).
2. Why should we be careful in making promises to God? (See Deut. 23:21-23; Ps. 76:11-12; 1 Sam. 1:11, 24-28).

TO THINK ABOUT AND DISCUSS

1. How can we demonstrate our awareness of God's holiness in the life of the church—particularly in worship? What specific changes might need to be made to your worship services in order to bring them more into line with the Bible's teaching and emphasis?
2. We are to listen before we speak (vv. 1-2). How can we put this into practice when we pray together?
3. What part should promises play in worship? How many have you made? How many have you kept?

8 From corruption to correction

(5:8-20)

'Money doesn't talk, it swears'. So said Bob Dylan in the 1960s. Thousands of years previously, the Preacher warned of the corruption that is inherent in the pursuit of money and the power it brings.

The corruption of man (vv. 8-17)

The fact of corruption (vv. 8-9)

In one of his sermons, A. W. Tozer tells the story of a ticket collector at a central railway station who was meticulous in examining everyone's ticket before he let them on to the platform. This often caused people to miss their trains. When regular customers complained to him, he pointed to the window of an office block overlooking the station. 'See that window,' he said. 'My boss works in that office and I never know if he is looking down at me!' Tozer told this story to illustrate the all-seeing eye of God.

Sadly, the Preacher is using the same picture in a different context.

It is not easy to understand his direct intent, for the terms he uses can have two meanings. The Hebrew can read *surprised* or *afraid*. Most commentators see this as corruption—the use of position in a hierarchy to exploit the poor. It can, however, also mean *indifference* to the poor. Those observing corruption are often as guilty as those participating. As one U. S. government official once said, 'The accomplice to the crime of corruption is frequently our own indifference.'

At the heart of it, however, is the fact of God's ultimate judgement on those who use their power to pervert the course of natural justice (Lev. 19:15; Deut. 24:17).

It is difficult to determine accurately what the Preacher means by, 'the king himself is served from the field'. On a positive note, it could mean, 'In spite of a corrupt bureaucracy, there is still a king overruling the land.' On the other hand, 'Even the king himself is part of the corrupt system that feeds him,' may well give us a more accurate picture of the Preacher's observations.

The one certain thing it does do is to acknowledge the reality of corruption in every area where one person has power over another.

The cause of corruption (v. 10)

It is virtually impossible for the average man to imagine immense wealth. Bill Gates, the creator of the Microsoft empire, is estimated to be worth nearly sixty billion dollars, making him the richest man in the world. The children of Sam Walton, founder of Walmart, are reputed to be worth over seventy-four billion dollars. There is little doubt that, comparatively, Solomon was as wealthy as any multi billionaire of our generation. Money attracts money, so they say, and the Queen of Sheba, no pauper herself, brought him a fortune. But there has to be a point where wealth becomes so vast it renders itself meaningless.

The apostle Paul echoes the Preacher's concern when he warns a young pastor of the dangers of wealth: 'But those who desire to be rich fall into temptation and a snare, and into many foolish and harmful lusts which drown men in destruction and perdition. For the love of money is a root of *all kinds of evil*' (1 Tim. 6:9-10, italics mine). The Preacher is issuing this warning to the wealthy—a continual close proximity to wealth may result in a passionate love affair with it!

The result of corruption (vv. 11-17)

DISSATISFACTION (V. 11)

Someone asked John D. Rockefeller, 'How much money does it take to satisfy a man?' Rockefeller replied, 'Just a little bit more than he has.' Increased wealth means increased expense. It also brings with it increased responsibility. We can see this in Solomon's lifestyle—his projects, marriages, servants, bodyguards consuming his fortune. Elvis Presley was born in a two-roomed shack in Tupelo, Mississippi. He died in a mansion across the state line in Memphis, Tennessee—with countless staff and minions—being pumped full of drugs to keep him going as he laboured to keep them in the lifestyle to which they had become accustomed. We can see this, too, in the instance of once proud boxers having one more fight... and then another... to pay off the debts of their lavish lifestyle or settle their tax bill.

SLEEPLESSNESS (V. 12)

Here is a comparison of lifestyles. One man exhausts himself physically, and whatever he eats is burned up in the process. His toil is hard, but simple and untroublesome and he sleeps well. The other man does not even have to break into a sweat, yet he cannot sleep. Indolence and indigestion may be the cause, but underlying this is something that cannot be cured by exercise and diet. He is a driven man, always having to keep ahead of the market. He stays late at his office, and is often the first to arrive the following morning. He is never far from his mobile phone—checking on the progress and health of his business. A fall in the market, the success of a competitor, or a wrong decision, may instantly rob him of a fortune. As Roland Murphy says, 'It seems as if the riches that the eyes contemplated so avidly now keep them from being closed in sleep.' [1]

ANXIETY (VV. 13-14)

Wealth can bring great anxiety. The Preacher calls this, 'a severe evil (*cf.* 5:16; 6:2). Such severity is echoed by the prophet, Nahum, when he writes, 'Your injury has no healing; your wound is severe' (Nahum 3:19). The hoarder has already lost his wealth in his mind. He always thinks that other hoarders are after it—he may even lose it in reality. He is a worried man—and he often looks it! Bernard Levin once described John Paul Getty as someone who 'went about looking like a man who cannot quite remember whether he remembered to turn the gas off before leaving home.'

A man must control greed in his mind before greed controls his mind! (Prov. 23:1-5).

FUTILITY (V. 15-17)

Many people work themselves into the ground in order to secure their future—but what future! Hands that frantically grasped hold of the riches of this world will be empty in the grave. The Preacher uses the term, 'carry away in his hand' to denote the material things that must remain behind, for we do not leave this world empty, but carry with us our character and integrity. These thoughts have a resonance in Psalm 49:10-12 and in Isaiah 5:8 where the prophets speaks of God's impending judgement on those who add 'house to house' and 'field to field'.

The stress and anxiety produced by unfettered materialism is simply 'labouring for the wind'. It will inevitably take its toll on health and happiness—even our eternal destiny (Mark 10:25; Matt. 13:22; Luke 18:18-23).

The correction of man (vv. 18-20)

The Preacher corrects the balance by making it clear that wealth is not inherently evil. The root of the problem is in the attitude of the heart and mind. Compare the vocabulary of the first section: 'loves silver', 'loves abundance', 'riches kept for their owner', 'laboured for the wind'—with 'God gives him', 'God has given riches and wealth', 'gift of God', and

'God keeps him busy with the joy of his heart.'

In the previous section wealth was viewed from an 'under the sun' perspective—now the Preacher raises his eyes and sees it in a different light. He now goes on to tell us what he has seen. Nothing has materially changed—but the attitude towards it has! Happiness comes when we recognize that all we possess belongs to God, because it comes from God. He even gives us the life in which we can possess things!

> If God chooses to bless us with wealth, it is for his glory! There are many people who have become wealthy and not been consumed by it.

The apostle Paul summarizes this for us when he writes, 'All things are yours... And you are Christ's, and Christ is God's' (1 Cor. 3:21-23). And he takes it further in his instructions to Timothy, 'Command those who are rich in this present age not to be haughty, nor to trust in uncertain riches but in the living God, who gives us richly all things to enjoy'—going on to urge them to 'be rich in good works, ready to give, willing to share.' (1 Tim. 6:17-18).

If God chooses to bless us with wealth, it is for his glory! There are many people who have become wealthy and not been consumed by it. Acknowledging that what they possess is a gift from God, they have sought to honour him in their stewardship. Joseph Rank spent a fortune in building churches and missions. The Cadbury brothers established a factory and a whole community that was years ahead of its time in providing good facilities and living accommodation for their workers. Samuel Colgate and Henry Heinz made sure that their businesses were built on ethical principles and contributed generously to God's work.

In 1831, Cyrus McCormick, an American farmer, invented a mechanical harvester. Six years later he went bankrupt. He lost his farm and everything he owned was put up for sale, with the exception of one item—his recent invention—which was deemed to be worthless by his creditors. In 1840 it went on sale, making him a multi-millionaire! But McCormick saw the need for a greater harvest and used part of his fortune to promote the evangelistic ministry of D. L. Moody.

These men had their priorities right. They enjoyed the benefits that their wealth gave them but were deeply conscious of the greater riches of Christ's Kingdom. The last will and testament of H. J. Heinz sums it up well: 'Looking forward to the time when my earthly career shall end, I desire to set forth at the very beginning of this will, as the most important thing in it, a confession of my faith in Jesus Christ as my Lord and Saviour; I also desire to bear witness to the fact that throughout my life, in which were the usual joys and sorrows, I have been wonderfully sustained by my faith in God. To him I attribute any success I may have obtained during my lifetime.'

It's all a matter of focus. If our emphasis is upon the gifts, then they will consume us and ultimately destroy us. If our emphasis is on the giver, the gifts are peripheral and can be used for his glory. This leads to true contentment and joy in the Lord (Phil. 4:11-13).

FOR FURTHER STUDY

1. What are the negative effects of the love of money (vv. 8-17. cf. Matt. 19:23-24; Mark 4:19; 10:17-22)?
2. What are the blessings of wealth (1 Tim. 6:17-19; 2 Cor. 8:1-24; 9:1-15)?

TO THINK ABOUT AND DISCUSS

1. Check your own attitude to material possessions. Are you suffering any of the symptoms of corruption recorded in vv. 11-17?
2. What is the best antidote for corruption (vv. 18-20)? How can this be applied?
3. Can you think of a person who has gained considerable wealth, but now seems to have lost a spiritual appetite, and maybe even seems to have lost a living faith in God? How might that person have avoided the negative side effects of wealth?

9 The future: futility or faith?

(6:1-12)

This passage naturally leads on from the previous one. It continues the Preacher's observations on the meaninglessness of materialism. It has been described as, 'A self-portrait, painted in words, of Solomon.'

As we have already noted, the Preacher makes use of three memorable phrases to describe his conclusions from his search for meaning and purpose in life. 'Under the sun' occurs thirty-five times within the book; 'vanity', twenty-five; and 'grasping for the wind', seven. All three occur in this section.

He is writing from the perspective of a man who has pursued happiness and fulfilment apart from God. Yet, at the same time, he is clearly someone who has known God, believes in God, and yet wandered away from him. He begins with two principles (vv. 1-2); illustrates and develops them (vv. 3-9); and finally, puts them into perspective (vv. 10-12).

The Principles (vv. 1-2)

There are two ways in which the original Hebrew of the first verse can be translated. It can simply mean 'common among men', but some place the emphasis on the magnitude of the evil rather than its frequency. For example, the NIV translates it as 'weighs heavily'. We could paraphrase a translation by incorporating both arguments as 'it frequently weighs heavily on men'. This is borne out in the two principles that follow in verse 2.

God is the provider of all good things

We can see this in Solomon's own experience. He had not sought wealth, but had only asked God for wisdom and knowledge, yet God had made him the richest man in his generation (2 Chr. 1:11-12). In his collection of Proverbs, he acknowledges this (Prov. 3:13-18), links his riches with righteousness (Prov. 8:18), and recognizes their source (Prov. 22:4). But, somewhere down the line, he has forgotten this—hence the self-portrait. The man who once recognized God's hand in all his blessings has faded into the wings (5:18-20). Now—centre stage—stands the self-made man.

Enjoyment is a gift from God

As we have already seen (in 5:19), the capacity to enjoy these things is also a gift from God—but in Ecclesiastes 6:2 this is withdrawn and the riches are enjoyed by a stranger! However, we are not told why he cannot enjoy them. The Jewish targum (oral paraphrase or interpretation of the Hebrew Old Testament) for this passage puts the blame on the man:

'But the Lord has not given him power, on account of sin, to enjoy it.' It may well be the case that sin or sickness prevents this particular rich man from enjoying his wealth, but it would not justify the Preacher's emphasis on God's sovereignty in the matter: 'Yet God does not give him power' (v. 2). Who is responsible for this man's calamity—himself, or God? Or both?

In the book of Job, the problem is compounded (Job 1:6-22). A wealthy man loses everything. It is clear that Satan is the perpetrator, and the Chaldeans his earthly agents—yet Job attributes it, without complaint, to the sovereign will of God: 'The LORD gave, and the LORD has taken away; Blessed be the name of the LORD' (v. 21). How can these three causes be reconciled? In his *Institutes*, John Calvin helps us by saying, 'The Lord designs to exercise the patience of his servant by adversity; Satan's plan is to drive him to despair; while the Chaldeans are bent on making unlawful gain by plunder... there is no inconsistency in attributing the same act to God, to Satan, and to man, while, from the difference in the end and mode of action, the spotless righteousness of God shines forth at the same time that the iniquity of Satan and man is manifested in its depravity.' [1] Or, as Thomas Watson put it, 'God can make a straight stroke with a crooked stick.' [2]

The man with the 'under the sun' mentality cannot see this, and therefore, unlike Job, he is driven to despair by his plight. He cannot find an earthly reason for his predicament—and he certainly cannot see a heavenly one! It is clear, from what the Preacher is saying, that a man cannot truly enjoy the gifts without the Giver.

The illustrations (vv. 3-9)

Time waits for no man (vv. 3-6)

When the former German Chancellor Conrad Ardeneur was an old man, he was examined by a physician who told him, 'I'm sorry sir, but I cannot make you any younger.'

'Don't worry,' said the Chancellor, 'just help me get a bit older!' Man vainly tries to fight back the advancing years, but time will always defeat him. Some have even resorted to cryogenics—having their bodies frozen —in the hope that we will one day have the capacity to raise the dead!

The Preacher pictures the futility of this by using an illustration that would be familiar to his Hebrew readers. A large family and a long life were considered to be typical signs of God's favour (Gen. 25:8; 35:9; Job 42:17; Ps. 127; Prov. 3:2). But abundant blessing, without the God who gives the ability to rejoice in it, draws the comparison of a Mega Methusulah and a stillborn child! Both will return to the darkness. The child, with no name, has not even glimpsed the sun, but he is better off than the man—whose tantalizing taste of the blessings that he has been unable to enjoy will mock him for eternity. As Warren Wiersbe puts it, 'What good is it for me to add years to my life *if I don't add life to my years?'* 3

> As Warren Wiersbe puts it, 'What good is it for me to add years to my life if I don't add life to my years?'

Swallowed up (vv. 7-9)

Some commentators have suggested that the word *mouth*—sometimes used in Hebrew poetry to denote Sheol, the place of the dead—links this section with the previous. But it would appear that the Preacher is referring to the general insatiability of human life. What applied to the rich man, applies equally to the poor (v. 8), caught up in the endless cycle of toiling to produce the food that will give him the energy to return to his toil—vainly maintaining a body that will eventually reach its demise (v. 7).

Even if a man were to enjoy his work and his food, he would still have to contend with a wandering imagination that will eventually make him discontented (v. 9). This proverbial statement has its parallels in our own culture—'A bird in the hand is worth two in the bush,' and 'The grass is greener in the other field.'

The perspective (vv. 10-12)

In the marginal note of the Massoretic text, this passage marks the middle of the book, and the turning point in the Preacher's thoughts. Tremper Longman III says, 'Qoheleth here leaves his explicit search for meaning and in the second half of the book focuses on advice and commentary about the future.' 4 He does this in two ways:

He restates the absolute sovereignty of God (vv. 10-11)

GOD HAS SPOKEN (V. 10)

Man is good at naming things (Gen. 2:19-20) and we can now

give names to diseases, even though we have yet to find the cure! But 'under the sun' there is nothing new—even though the names have been changed to protect the ignorant! Yet the sovereign Word of God is creative and powerful. God spoke, and brought everything into being. 'God said' occurs ten times in Genesis 1. This is echoed in the New Testament (Heb. 1:1,2; 4:12; Matt. 8:8). God tells us through Isaiah that his Word shall 'accomplish what I please' (Isa. 55:11).

GOD HAS COMPLETE FOREKNOWLEDGE (V. 10)

The use of the Hebrew *adam* seems to indicate that the Preacher is referring to the naming of man by God—echoing the words, 'For he knows ... that we are dust.'(Ps. 103:14; *cf.* Eccles. 3:20; 12:7). The Psalmist speaks of such foreknowledge (Ps. 103); Jeremiah was set aside as a prophet before he was even born (Jer. 1:5); Nathaniel was astounded that Jesus saw him under a fig tree, even though he was still a long way off (John 1:48-49). For the ungodly, the foreknowledge of God is a daunting prospect; but for the godly it is their greatest comfort, 'For it is known that he is man' (*cf.* Ps. 139).

WHO ARE WE TO ARGUE? (VV. 10-11)

The sovereignty of God is indisputable—how can puny man 'contend with him who is mightier than he'? The apostle Paul makes the same kind of statement: 'O man, who are you to reply against God? Will the thing formed say to him who formed it, "Why have you made me like this?"' (*cf.* Isa. 45:9-12).

Verse 11 can refer to speech or possessions. The NIV renders it 'The more the words, the less the meaning, and how does that profit anyone?' Both give an incisive picture of man's futile attempts to elevate himself to godlike status. The increase of knowledge, wealth or status do not give him any kind of sovereignty—they just increase the vanity! In effect—it's all talk!

The future is beyond man's knowledge and understanding (v. 12)

In his amazing story '1984' George Orwell writes, 'Who controls the past controls the future. Who controls the present controls the past.' [5] It is evident that man has been unable to exercise any control over his destiny, yet he persistently seeks to discover what the future holds. Lost in the shadow of his own ignorance, he hangs on the words of anyone who claims prophetic vision. Presidents have turned to astrologers and numerologists; hard-bitten businessmen have made decisions on the turn of a Tarot card—all in a vain attempt to crack the code that will unlock tomorrow. 'What vanity,' declares the Preacher. 'Who can tell a man what will happen after him under the sun?' There is no ghost of Christmas past, present or future—destiny lies in the hand of a sovereign God.

Summary

The Preacher is like a man who has fallen into despair, and knows what has caused his fall. He cries out to those who have yet to fall, 'Do not follow me!' We do him an injustice, however, if we marvel at his poetry, or nod our heads in agreement with his observations of life 'under the sun' and do not heed his warning and stop 'grasping for the wind'.

FOR FURTHER STUDY

1. Read the following passages: Heb. 1:3; Isa. 55:11; Matt. 8:8; Psalm 103. How do they relate to Eccles. 6:2, 10-12?

2. Read Job 1:1-22. What is the cause of Job's plight? How does it help us interpret Eccles. 6:1-2?

TO THINK ABOUT AND DISCUSS

1. How would viewing material possessions as a gift from God change our attitude to them?

2. Look at the illustrations in vv. 3-9. Can you add to them from your own life and experience?

3. The Preacher is deeply concerned about the future (v. 12). What is your attitude towards your future and that of all you leave behind?

4. What would be your response to a neighbour or work colleague who came to you to ask whether it was all right to get the help of an astrologist in order to predict the future?

5. How does this section clarify the biblical teaching on 'health and wealth' as sometimes presented by those who teach that it is the will of God only for his children to enjoy health and wealth all the time?

10 Words of wisdom

(7:1-8:1)

Here is a passage full of wise advice gleaned from the Preacher's observations of life. He moves from the negative to the positive by listing things that are worthwhile. His advice is conveyed in different ways: comparison, warning, and consideration.

Comparison

Comparison has always been a helpful means by which we can evaluate something. When purchasing something, we compare products and prices before we buy. Even Shakespeare uses this means when writing of the beloved, 'Shall I compare thee to a summer's day!' The Preacher concludes that some things are better than others, as he lays his comparisons before his readers in the following verses.

Honour is better than luxury (v. 1)

The opening words of this verse have their parallel in Solomon's collection of proverbs: 'A good name is to be chosen rather than great riches, loving favour rather than silver and gold' (Prov. 22:1). Why does the Preacher use *perfume* as his comparable object rather than *silver* and *gold*? There could be two reasons.

A good name was highly valued in Hebrew culture (Job 18:17; Prov. 10:7)—perfume was also highly regarded (Ps. 45:7; 133; Amos 6:6; Matt. 6:17; 26:7), and often used as a metaphor for anointing by God. But the Preacher is using them to represent the inward values and the outward appearance. The reputation of a man is transparent, but perfume can be used as a cover-up. Jesus referred to the Pharisees as 'whitewashed sepulchres'.

The *perfume* may be linked to the second part of the verse. When the woman anointed Jesus with expensive perfume, he responded by saying that she was anointing him for his burial (Matt. 26:6-13). The poor man may not have expensive perfume applied to his body but a good name will count for more!

Death is better than birth (v. 1)

As a man's inner character is far better than any outward fragrance, so his funeral and not his birthday party will reveal his true value. If a man dies with a good reputation, it will remain and even be enhanced by the passage of time, for while he is still alive that reputation can be harmed. And even if he has a bad reputation, the day of his death is better—for he can do no more harm, cause no more hurt, suffer no more shame. And, for the Christian, the words are certainly true. At birth we are brought into a world of sin and sorrow; at death we are delivered from it! The apostle Paul writes, 'For to me, to live is Christ, and to die is gain' (Phil. 1:21). For all, in the mind of the Preacher, death is the ultimate escape from life's oppression and meaninglessness.

Mourning is better than feasting (v. 2)

> Modern people do not even like to think about death—but the house of mourning, the seat in the crematorium, or the place at the graveside confront us with our mortality.

Modern people do not even like to think about death—but the house of mourning, the seat in the crematorium, or the place at the graveside confront us with our mortality. It is easier to be elsewhere, but it is better to be here, where we learn to 'number our days, that we may gain a heart of wisdom' (Ps. 90:12). The passing of a loved on cuts us to the heart, but often it is the surgeon's scalpel that removes the cancer of false promise that keeps us 'under the sun'. The wound may be deep but, if we listen to the voice of God, we will meet with the one who was 'wounded for our transgressions' (Isa. 53:5)—who speaks of his blessedness for 'those who mourn' and promises his comfort (Matt. 5:4).

Sorrow is better than laughter (vv. 3-4)

The theme continues by broadening the picture to sorrow

and laughter and then returning to the theme of death and mourning. It may be a cliché, but our disappointments are often God's appointments. Our fallen human nature will barely allow us a thought for God during times of great blessing, but we will soon turn to him when things begin to go wrong. The Hebrew translated as *sorrow* can also mean *anger* or *frustration*. The Preacher includes both elements in Eccles. 5:17 when he says, 'And he has much sorrow and sickness and anger.' This describes the intensity of grief or bitter disappointment. It may well be that the latter half of the verse refers to those who are not just temporally made sad, for it is far better than laughter only when it shatters the illusion of temporal happiness and turns man's heart and mind to God. Elsewhere, the Bible contrasts both kinds of sorrow: 'Now I rejoice, not that you were made sorry, but that your sorrow led to repentance. For you were made sorry in a godly manner... For godly sorrow produces repentance to salvation, not to be regretted; but the sorrow of the world produces death' (2 Cor. 7:9-10).

Rebuke is better than praise (vv. 5-6)

In the book of Proverbs, Solomon writes, 'Faithful are the wounds of a friend, but the kisses of an enemy are deceitful' (Prov. 27:6). Verse 5 carries the same theme. The American politician and diplomat, Adlai Stevenson, once remarked, 'Flattery is all right—if you don't inhale it!' Praise can be a heady drug, but it is rarely any use to us. The crackling thorns under the pot make an impressive display of intense fire, but never last long enough to produce a meal. When we receive the 'rebuke of the wise' we may feel that we are being roasted, but in the end it produces something that will nourish and sustain us.

Patience is better than pride (vv. 7-8)

It is difficult to understand exactly what the Preacher is saying here. But it would appear that he is giving us a picture of the vulnerability of wisdom. On one hand, oppression or extortion can cloud a man's judgement; and on the other, a bribe will distort it. As Tremper Longman says, 'The former makes the wise person a fool by surrendering control of life to another; the latter clouds one's judgement by introducing bias.' [1] Amid the pressures of life, it would be easy to submit to either, but a larger picture of the situation will help us to resist (v. 8).

Wisdom is better than wealth (vv. 11-12)

Wisdom and wealth are not mutually exclusive. God has blessed many with both. But wealth without wisdom offers no shelter. It is like a straw roof that will soon blow away or be consumed by fire. Whereas wisdom without wealth 'preserves the life of its possessor' (v. 12, NIV).

Warning

The Preacher introduces four warnings in this chapter, all preceded by the words, 'Do not.' In an earlier book *Depression: a rescue plan* I have expanded on these as essentials for psycholgical health and wellbeing. [2]

Do not react when you can respond (v. 9)

Man is a living organism, not a machine. Machines react—

man responds—or so he should! We have a God-given autonomic nervous system that reacts to danger or need, but hasty reaction is inappropriate where a considered response is called for.

In this particular instance, the Preacher is referring to anger, but the principle can be applied to all non-threatening circumstances. 'Do you see a man hasty in his words? There is more hope for the fool than for him' (Prov. 29:20; see also 19:3; 21:5). In the New Testament, even the city clerk at Ephesus sees the wisdom in this (Acts 19:36).

We all have a tendency to jump to conclusions and we often make the mistake of completing the picture before we have all the information. How many relationships have been damaged because explanations were not allowed to be completed, or actions have been misconstrued?

Do not dwell on the past (v. 10)

Looking back is part of true perspective. The Bible commands us to do this (Isa. 46:8-9; 1 Cor. 11:24-25), but we must not dwell on the past and make unhealthy and unwise comparisons between present circumstances and past events (Ps. 42:4). We are not to dwell on past blessings, other than to give thanks to God, or to remind ourselves of his providential care. To do so is to blind ourselves to what God is doing in our lives at this present moment. It is far easier for us to look back and see what God has done than to detect his purpose in our present circumstances.

Past experiences still retain great power within us. If you want to test this hypothesis, just try remembering one of your most embarrassing moments! Have you started to blush yet?

Do not be extreme (vv. 16-18)

In some ways, the Christian life seems to be filled with excesses. Our righteousness is to exceed the righteousness of the Pharisees (Matt. 5:20); we are to be 'exceedingly glad' when people persecute us (Matt. 5:12); God has given us, 'exceedingly great and precious promises' (2 Peter 1:4), and has promised to do 'exceedingly abundantly above all that we ask or think' (Eph. 3:20). The Preacher, however, warns us of the danger of the wrong kind of excess.

The whole of God's creation is wonderfully balanced. 'While the earth remains, seedtime and harvest, and cold and heat, and winter and summer, and day and night, shall not cease' (Gen. 8:22). The Christian life is a balance of weakness and strength (2 Cor. 12:9-10); labour and rest (Luke 13:24; Matt. 11:28-30); gain and loss (Phil. 3:7); and shadow and sunshine (Ps. 30:5; Rev. 7:14-17). The mountain-top experience of the disciples was balanced by the need that awaited them in the valley (Matt. 17; Mark 9).

We must learn to be balanced in the way that we perceive the circumstances of our lives. There is a danger of making sweeping generalizations about things.

Do not be oversensitive (vv. 21-22)

Our perception is impaired when we become oversensitive to what people say or do. A thoughtless word or action can often cause a person to burst into tears. Can we do anything about this? We can take preventative measures that will dissipate its power over us. We all get hurt by criticism or by what people say about us. We must not, however, take these things to heart. We have already discovered that it is a human trait to speak critically about others, especially when they are not there. This is why the Preacher goes on to say, 'For many times, also, your heart has known that even you have cursed others' (Eccles. 7:22). Many of us would be ashamed if others knew of the things we said about them when they were not there. If we had to explain our action, we would say that we either spoke in a fit of anger; or we did not really mean what we said; or we were simply having a bad day and did not have a good word to say about anyone. This may well have been true, but the damage will have been done. We must beware of the power of the tongue (James 3). The thing we must bear in mind is that when people speak ill of us, their explanation would probably be the same! If we are over-sensitive, we will dwell on every word. If we have received the information through a third party, we will dwell on every misquotation!

> We must beware of the power of the tongue (James 3)

Consideration

Consider what God has done (vv. 13-15)

As we consider the providential care of God, we soon become aware that it is not always as straightforward as we might expect. The crookedness and injustice of so many things we encounter, especially when we consider the problem of evil, seem to contradict the justice and sovereignty of God. Theologians and philosophers have long tried to 'straighten out' these things, but can never do so to man's satisfaction.

The Preacher does not even attempt this for, as Michael Eaton puts it, '[He] aims neither to abolish nor even explain life's abnormalities, but to enable one to live with them.'[3] God has sovereign rule over everything—and will work everything to his own purpose for his glory and the good of his people (Rom. 8:18-30).

Consider what sin has done (vv. 19-29)

Whereas it may be difficult to understand the providence of God in allowing the unjust to prosper—the root of that injustice has a simple explanation—sin. The Preacher is honest about the struggle that he has experienced in this area. The touchstone for his evaluation of life has been wisdom (vv. 19, 23), but he has only partially succeeded (vv. 23-24). He has approached it almost mathematically, trying to tally up his observations. He has scarcely found a wise man—and has yet to find a wise woman (v. 28)! The Preacher is not a misogynist (9:9; Prov. 12:4; 14:1), but he warns of the snares of unbridled lust (v. 26). But there is one thing he seems sure of, and that is the perversity of the human heart (v. 29). His observations have, in the end, accorded with God's evaluation of man (v. 20, cf. Isa. 53:6; Rom. 3:12, 23; 1 John 1:8).

Summary

True wisdom lights up the face of a man or woman (8:1). An elderly lady was once asked what cosmetics she used to maintain her beautiful complexion. She replied, 'For my lips, truth; for my voice, prayer; for my eyes, pity; for my hands, charity; for my figure, uprightness; and for my heart, love!'

All this is to be found in the one who is the personification of wisdom—Jesus Christ (Prov. 8:22-31; John 1:1-14).

FOR FURTHER STUDY

1. Read Matt. 5:3-12. Does this give you a clearer understanding of the Preacher's comparisons?

2. What is God's evaluation of man (Isa. 53:6; Rom. 3:12-25; 1 John 1:8-9)? Notice how his mercy is is declared alongside his judgement.

TO THINK ABOUT AND DISCUSS

1. Take a psychological health check from this passage. Do you react to issues instead of responding (v. 9)? Do you dwell too much on the past (v. 10)? Is your thinking properly balanced (vv. 16-18)? Are you oversensitive (vv. 21-22)?

2. Take time to consider the two personal issues that the Preacher presents to you. Consider what God has done for you (vv. 13-15). Consider what sin has done to you (vv. 19-29). In what way or ways does this make you any wiser?

3. How would you use the teaching of this passage to help an overly sensitive person to develop a more realistic approach to life?

11 Obedience to authority

(8:1-8)

The passage that lies before us deals with how we are to respond when we are in situations where we are interacting with those in authority over us. We see this also in the New Testament advice of Paul and Peter, and the example of Jesus before Pilate.

The first problem we have to face is a technical one. Where do we begin our exposition of this section? We closed the last chapter on 8:1, following the NKJV outline. However, a number of commentators see 8:1 as the beginning of this section rather than the end of the preceding one. This should not trouble us, for this verse forms a natural link between the two.

Principle (v. 1)

Having travelled thus far with the Preacher, it is hard to imagine him as being the personification of his statement in this verse. His search for a wise man or woman has been futile, and his own wisdom has only frustrated his attempts at finding out the meaning and purpose of life. It is difficult to picture a smile on his face as he writes these words. One commentator has suggested that this is 'a sarcastic explanation of frustration' linking the two sections together. Whatever the Preacher's state of mind at the time of writing, he is certainly expressing truth that is firmly rooted in other Scripture passages.

Although he has struggled to find a wise man, God has placed such men in positions of authority and influence that this section deals with. Both Joseph and Daniel rose to great prominence through their God-given ability to interpret things (Gen. 41:37-45; Dan. 5:29-6:3). Jesus taught his disciples, 'Now when they bring you to the synagogues and magistrates and authorities, do not worry about how or what you should answer, or what you should say. For the Holy Spirit will teach you in that very hour what you ought to say' (Luke 12:11-12). When the apostle Paul was brought before Felix and Drusilla, his words made them tremble (Acts 24:25), and his testimony before Agrippa brought the response, 'You almost persuade me to become a Christian' (Acts 26:28).

The shining face was a testimony of God's favour. Aaron blessed the people with the words, 'The LORD make his face shine upon you' (Num. 6:25). Moses' face shone while he was talking with God (Exod. 34:29; 2 Cor. 3:7), and Stephen's beatific visage was plain to see as he answered his accusers (Acts 6:15).

Practice (vv. 2-4)

The place of proper obedience (v. 2)

A graffito prominent in the 1970s said, 'Don't bother to vote—the government always get in!' This sums up the cynicism and apathy of many voters towards the governments they have previously elected. In a totalitarian society, these sentiments may be replaced by fear and dread, but the truth is that no government is popular with the majority of its subjects!

The Preacher tells us to 'keep the king's commandment for the sake of your oath to God.' This oath clearly indicates the relationship between government and God. All government—whether just or unjust, democratic or despotic—comes under the providential care of God for the good of man. Our obedience to God is verified by our obedience to the secular authority that he refers to as his 'minister to you for good' (Rom. 13:1-7). Anarchy is always worse than bad government.

Jesus said, 'Render to Caesar the things that are Caesar's, and to God the things that are God's' (Mark 12:17), and Peter exhorts us to 'submit yourselves to every ordinance of man for the Lord's sake' (1 Peter 2:13-17).

The place of proper respect (vv. 3-4)

Dealing with any kind of bureaucracy has its pitfalls. One man's decision, anywhere along the chain of command, can spell success or failure. The Preacher's advice on behaviour before a monarch is equally applicable to situations we may encounter on any bureaucratic level. We achieve nothing by exasperating those in authority—neither will we get a sympathetic hearing from one to whom we have been discourteous.

We must not storm out when advice we have given or a request we have made is turned down. Neither are we to enter into any plot against the person who has refused us, however unjustly we may feel we have been treated. The Preacher has taken his case 'to the top', and advises those who do so to show proper respect to the one

> We achieve nothing by exasperating those in authority —neither will we get a sympathetic hearing from one to whom we have been discourteous.

in authority. He also teaches us not to continue in a cause that is patently unacceptable. In the end we will fail miserably because, 'he does whatever pleases him'. God placed Esther, a lowly orphan, in the court of the Persian king, Ahasuerus, to further the cause of the Jews. Her deportment and respect for the monarch, and her behaviour in his presence, exemplify what the Preacher is saying (*cf.* Esth. 5:1-8).

Promise (vv 5-6a)

This section appears to contradict what precedes it, but, in fact, it supplies the balance. The overruling factor is reintroduced—we are under the providential care of God. (v. 5a). Paul was executed by the Romans, yet he was able to write of the authorities of his day, 'For rulers are not a terror to good works, but to evil. Do you want to be unafraid of the authority? Do what is good, and you will have praise from the same' (Rom. 13:3). We have already seen how Joseph, Daniel, and Esther were placed in positions of prominence by God and were given discernment that would enable them to fulfil God's will for their people. But their obedience to the king was always subject to their obedience to God.

The Christian has long been faced with the dilemma of knowing when it is right to remain silent and when it is right to protest. The Preacher provides the answer: 'For every matter there is a time and judgement' (v. 6). The wise man has his heart attuned to God and will know God's timing and judgement in this matter—he will know what to say and when to say it! Jonathan boldly stood up for David before King Saul (1 Sam. 19:4-6) and Nathan was able to admonish David without fear of retribution (2 Sam. 12).

Timing is essential to every area of life. The golfer or the cricketer who is out of form is not 'timing' the ball right; the footballer who mistimes his tackle commits a bad foul; the top comedian is said to be one who times his jokes perfectly; and the Prime Minister is urged to call a general election 'at the right time'. The Preacher has already advocated that there is a right time for everything (Eccles. 3:1-8). The God who controls the destiny of man has a perfect time for everything. His own Son came into this world only 'when the fulness of the time had come' (Gal. 4:4).

Prospect (vv. 6b-8)

Man's prospects are in the hand of God. For the man with the 'under the sun' perspective, this brings great anxiety and frustration that the Preacher describes as, 'the misery of man.' He has previously described our inability to know what lies before us (3:21; 6:12). The king may exercise total power over his subjects but he, like them, is subject to the same blindness to future events—even the wisest of men is frustrated by his ignorance of such things. As one commentator puts it, 'A wise person is someone who is able to make competent decisions that fit a particular situation. An important component of this ability is an intuition concerning the future results of a decision. But here such a possibility is denied.' [1] Christ wept over Jerusalem because he foresaw its future and was grieved by the unwillingness of his generation to listen to God's messengers and heed their words (Matt. 23:37)—they had even refused to listen to him:'If you had known, even you, especially in this your day, the things that make for your peace! But now they are hidden from your eyes' (Luke 19:42). The Preacher directs us to four areas where all men are powerless:

Powerlessness over the spirit

Some have translated the word *spirit* as 'wind' or 'the breath of life'. The spirit of man has been breathed into him by the breath of God (Gen. 2:7). It is God alone who is in control of his generation and regeneration. In the upper room, the risen Christ breathed on his disciples and said, 'Receive the Holy Spirit' (John 20:22). The picture of regeneration given to Nicodemus was of the wind blowing wherever it pleases—'So,' said Jesus, 'is everyone who is born of the Spirit' (John 3:8). A man can exercise no control over the fate of his spirit. His body will return to dust and his 'spirit will return to God who gave it' (Eccles. 12:7).

Powerlessness over death

This naturally follows on from the previous sentence. No man has control over the day of his death—even the suicidal are victims of their circumstances, 'And as it is appointed for men to die once, but after this the judgement' (Heb. 9:27). Man's helplessness in this matter is alleviated by God's grace—for the writer of Hebrews goes on to say, 'So Christ was offered once to bear the sins of many. To those who eagerly wait for him he will appear a second time, apart from sin, for salvation' (Heb. 9:28).

No release from war

Ever the realist, the Preacher may simply be referring to wars that occur as a result of man's sinful heart. There has never been a moment in history when there has not been war here on earth. But, by referring to 'that war', he may be citing the continual battle between life and death. Death appears constant, throughout our lives, as the great enemy of man—taking our loved ones, shattering our dreams, hovering like a dark cloud over our days here on earth. There is no respite in this battle and no one is dismissed from its front line.

Wickedness will not deliver

A man may be able to lie and cheat his way out of many difficulties in life, but in death, all his efforts will fail. Extortion and exploitation will not add one hour to his miserable life. Despots may stash up great hordes of wealth before they flee into exile, but there is no exile from the Judgement Day of God. What a grim prospect for those who thought they were powerful 'under the sun'!

The Bible teaches that people's wickedness is rooted in their unbelief. Those who reject God's grace and mercy will share the same fate as the despot (John 3:18-21).

Our ultimate authority is God. Obedience to those that he has appointed over us is counted as obedience to him—but whoever we are, prince or pauper, we cannot escape his judgement and condemnation unless we obey his appointed King over all creation, Jesus Christ.

FOR FURTHER STUDY

1. Look at the lives of Joseph (Gen. 39 - 41) and Daniel (Dan. 1 - 2), and note how God used them to bring blessing upon Egypt and Babylon.

2. Why are we to be obedient to human authority (vv. 2-8. cf. Rom. 13:1-7; 1 Peter 2:13-17)?

TO THINK ABOUT AND DISCUSS

1. What are the limitations of human authority (v. 8)?

2. In what situation would you believe it right to disobey human authority (Matt. 22:21; Acts 4:13-22; cf. Dan. 3; 6:1-23)?

3. Can you think of any recent situation in international affairs where anarchy has (even temporarily) replaced the rule of government? What were some of the features you can list? How does this illustrate the principles expounded in this section of Ecclesiastes?

12 Life's not fair, but God is good

(8:9-17)

It is patently obvious that life is not fair! Some people seem to sail through untroubled—yet for others, one problem or tragedy seems to follow another. These are the facts of life, 'under the sun'. The Preacher addresses them realistically and shows his readers how he has come to terms with them.

In 1990 the National League for Democracy was overwhelmingly elected as the government of Burma (Myanmar)—taking 392 of the 485 contested seats. The people of the new government were barred by the military regime from taking their seats in parliament, their offices were raided, and their leaders were exiled, imprisoned or killed. Their spokesperson, and icon of the Burmese people, Aung San Suu Kyi, was placed under house arrest—where she remains to this day. Burma has degenerated into an economic wasteland, enduring United Nations sanctions as a result of its human rights record.

The powerful are not always just (v. 9)

As in the previous chapter, this verse forms a bridge between the two sections. The Preacher has been referring to the power of rulers. He introduces his next theme about the injustices of life by referring to the abuse of that power. His application to the task in hand is intense, as he muses upon the things that he has observed within the hierarchies of society.

The term 'to his own hurt' can also be translated, 'to their hurt'. It is unlikely that the Preacher is referring to personal damage done to the tyrant by his own actions. Although in eternity he will be brought to judgement, the context of this passage suggests that the Preacher is referring to the temporal pain suffered by those who are the victims of his unfairness.

Death does not redress the balance (v. 10)

This passage is one of the most enigmatic in the book, and it would be foolish for an expositor to claim that he has fully understood it. The best we can do is to put it into context and try to get to the heart of what the Preacher is saying. The overriding theme seems to be that the wicked do not appear to get what they deserve—even in death.

God had decreed that all men should have a dignified and honourable burial. Even criminals and enemies were afforded this right (Deut. 21:22-23; 2 Sam. 17:23; Josh. 8:29). The Preacher has observed the funeral services of the just and the unjust and all are treated with the same honour.

The wicked and the holy place

What does the Preacher mean when he refers to the wicked as those 'who had come and gone from the place of holiness'? He could be referring to the burial service itself—with the body carried from the place of worship to the graveside. This is unlikely.

We could read it as an expression of satisfaction that the wicked have now departed from the presence of God, to await the fate they justly deserve. This is unlikely, too, for in this same verse he refers to what he sees as 'vanity'.

It is more likely that he is referring to the city of Jerusalem itself—the very place where these injustices have been committed. We could take it further by suggesting that he has also observed their observance of the trapping of religion in life in their coming and going from the Temple, yet their being devoid of true religion in their dealings with others (James 1:27). Jesus had the same perspective of the Pharisees (Matt. 23:27).

Forgotten or praised?

Scholars are divided over the correct translation of the Hebrew that is rendered here as *forgotten*, but in the NIV as *praised*. Those who prefer *forgotten* suggest that the Preacher is no longer referring to the unjust, but the just. The context, however, seems to suggest that this is not the case. Those who favour *praise* make a slight emendation of the Hebrew—and the context seems to favour their view. What is galling for the Preacher is to hear the eulogies of men who have blatantly acted unjustly resounding in the very city of their exploits.

We are taught, not to 'speak ill of the dead', and out of proper respect we acquiesce. But it is hard to sit and listen to the praise heaped upon those whose lives have not deserved it, and attend the 'Christian funeral' of someone who has shown no interest in the things of God. We sometimes wonder whether we have gone to the right funeral. In doing so, however, we are not to pass judgement, but to hope that, unknown to us, the person has come to peace with God through Jesus Christ.

Common grace seems to make the position worse (v. 11)

Man is a creature of the moment—tomorrow never comes! It is amazing how we have the capacity to dismiss the consequences of our actions simply because they are not imminent. It is not the moral aspect of law that makes man obey—it is the threat of punishment. If punishment is not meted out, or for some reason delayed, the law is of little effect. Companies and individuals flout laws simply because they are not enforced, knowing that even though they are guilty, they will 'get away with it'. The Preacher gets to the root of the matter by referring to 'the heart of the sons of men' being 'fully set in them to do evil'. The delay in punishment encourages the sinful heart in its rebellion. He is troubled by this, for he sees it as a great injustice.

> It is amazing how we have the capacity to dismiss the consequences of our actions simply because they are not imminent.

What makes matters seem worse is that what applies to the justice meted out by men also seems to apply to that given by God. This has perplexed people in all generations: 'How can a God of righteousness allow the wicked to prosper? He has declared his judgement upon them, but it never seems to come.' Peter explains this when he says, 'The Lord is not slack concerning his promise, as some count slackness, but is longsuffering towards us, not willing that any should perish but that all should come to repentance' (2 Peter 3:9). God's common grace to all people delays their judgement with the intent that they should repent and believe the gospel, for one day, in his sovereign plan, that judgement will fall (2 Peter 3:10).

In 'under the sun' thinking, there is no justice—life's not fair. But what follows takes our understanding above the sun and gives it an eternal perspective.

Keep the eternal perspective (vv. 12-14)

When faced with injustice all around us, we must hold on to the promise that God has triumphed through his Son, and that evil will be punished in the end. Why must we hold on to this great hope? The Preacher answers the question for us in verse 14.

There are two ways of looking at this verse: Firstly, we can see again the unfairness of life but there is also a glimmer of light that comes to its full radiance in the gospel. It speaks of 'righteous men who get what the wicked deserve' (NIV), and 'wicked men who get what the righteous deserve' (NIV). Even acts of justice and mercy will not spare us from eternal punishment if we reject Christ. Such acts can never make a man righteous before God, for even though he enables us to perform them, they will not change the inherent unrighteousness of our hearts (Rom. 3:10,20; Isa. 64:6). The repentant sinner, however will be treated as a righteous person—not in his or her own righteousness, but that of Jesus Christ (Rom. 4:13-25). This is nonsense 'under the sun' but is the essence of God's justice and mercy.

Do not be reduced to cynicism or despair (v. 15)

This is the fourth time that the Preacher has expressed this sentiment, 'eat, drink, and be merry'. It is used elsewhere in the Bible in a different context. Isaiah pictures it as a sign of rebellion against the commands of God (Isa. 22:13), and the irresponsibility of leaders (Isa. 56:12). Jesus uses it when he describes a man who is self-satisfied and has given no thought for his eternal destiny (Luke 12:19). Paul describes someone who has no hope in the resurrection and resigns himself to blotting out his sense of futility (1 Cor. 15:32).

It is tempting to give in to cynicism or despair as we observe the injustices of life under the sun. The Preacher, however, uses the phrase in a positive way. On each occasion he is emphasizing the hand of God at work. Even in the midst of unfairness and injustice, we are to recognize the positive elements of our lives that are, in themselves, a gift from God (5:18). He has previously taught that the pleasures we derive from even the simplest things are 'from the hand of God' (2:24-26). The good that comes from our labour is to be recognized as 'the gift of God' (3:12-13), and he even goes on to say of a man that 'God keeps him busy with the joy of his heart' (5:20).

Peter learned a valuable lesson when instructed, 'What God has cleansed you must not call common' (Acts 10:15), and Paul tells us, 'Therefore, whether you eat or drink, or whatever you do, do all to the glory of God' (1 Cor. 10:31).

Hengstenberg paraphrases it in this way: 'Joy is a godly cheerfulness and serenity of the soul; since the just man, though he may suffer from the vanities of this world, which are common to all, keeps his soul free from vain cares, calm through faith in God, and hence cheerful and ready in the performance of its duties; so that he eats, drinks and rejoices, i.e. enjoys what God has given him, in a calm, cheerful and fitting manner.' [1]

Trust in God's wisdom (vv. 16-17)

Left with an 'under the sun' perspective, man finds it impossible to come to terms with the unfairness of life, as he observes 'the business that is done on earth'—it only gives him sleepless nights. Even his futile attempts at redressing the balance through the law courts only increase his frustration at the sense of injustice as he sees large corporations and even governments hiring expensive attorneys to further their ends. Justice often seems to be the last thing on the agenda! When the state of Georgia, America, was founded in 1732, the governor, James Edward Oglethorpe, introduced regulations to maintain the harmony within the community and with their Indian neighbours. Along with slavery and alcohol, *lawyers*, too, were forbidden!

There is no solution to the problem, but the Preacher does not leave us in despair. He reminds us that all these things are the work of God. The answer to man's frustration is divine revelation. God has revealed that his ways are far beyond us (Isa. 55:8-9), and urges us to forsake pointless speculation and to turn to him (Isa. 55:6-7). As Matthew Henry puts it, 'Leaving the Lord to clear up all the difficulties in his own time, we may cheerfully enjoy the comforts, and bear up under the trials of life; while peace of conscience and joy in the Holy Ghost will abide in us through all outward changes, and when flesh and heart shall fail.' [2]

FOR FURTHER STUDY

1. What are the most common forms of injustice people have to face (vv. 9-14)?
2. The New Testament church was conceived and grew in a society where injustice prevailed. How were they instructed to live (1 Peter 2:18-25; Eph. 6:5-9; Luke 6:27-36)?

TO THINK ABOUT AND DISCUSS

1. How would you answer the question, 'If God is just, why does he continue to allow injustice to prevail' (vv. 11-13, cf. 2 Peter 3:1-13)?
2. What is the overriding factor that gives us hope in the midst of injustice (vv. 16-17)? How can you apply this?
3. Do you know of believers who are presently experiencing injustice? Does the manner in which they are bearing it demonstrate the wisdom and teaching of the Scriptures?

13 Pessimism and preparation

(9:1-18)

The first part of this chapter has been referred to as the most pessimistic passage in the entire book. But it ends on a more optimistic note, preparing us for the positive elements that will follow in the next three chapters.

Destiny (vv. 1-6)

The Preacher reflects on all he has learned from his observations and personal experiments with life under the sun, and these reveal great truth and error about the nature of salvation. It is in this passage that the 'under the sun' perspective meets true biblical faith head on.

The fact of death

'Perhaps the whole root of our trouble, the human trouble, is that we will sacrifice all the beauty of our lives, will imprison ourselves in totems, taboos, crosses, blood sacrifices, steeples, mosques, races, armies, flags, nations, in order to deny the fact of death, which is the only fact we have.' [1] So wrote the American author James Baldwin.

It is this fact that is determining the Preacher's nihilistic conclusions. He has observed the unfairness of life, seen its injustices but, at the end of it all, the grave is the great leveller: 'Everything occurs alike to all' (v. 2) and 'that one thing happens to all' (v. 3).

In this section the Preacher expresses two great truths about death and eternity, but goes on to make a grave error of judgement.

God is sovereign (v. 1)

The fate of man is ultimately in the hand of God. The hand or arm is a biblical metaphor denoting power. It is used about 200 times in the Old Testament to refer to the sovereign power of God. It refers to his creative power (Ps. 19:1; Isa. 48:13); his judgmental power (Isa. 19:16; Zech. 2:9); his saving power (Exod. 14:31, literally, 'hand with which the LORD worked'; (Ps. 78:42); and his protective power (Ezra 7:9; Neh. 2:18).

In the New Testament we see the picture of Christ in his creative power (Heb. 1:10. *cf.* v. 2); coming to sift the wheat from the chaff (Matt. 3:4); reaching out his hand in cleansing and healing (Luke 5:13; Mark 8:23). The Christian's hope is in the hand of God: 'Therefore humble yourselves under the mighty hand of God, that he might exalt you in due time, casting all your care upon him, for he cares for you' (1 Peter 5:6-7).

A man's works will not determine his destiny (vv. 2-6)

The Preacher speaks of death as an evil, for 'that one thing happens to all' (v. 3). It seems so unjust that, 'under the sun', the good and the bad share the same fate. Their works, whether good or bad have the same reward—oblivion! There is only one division between men—the dead and the living. The dead will be forgotten, and 'nevermore will have a share in anything done under the sun' (v. 6). Death closes the book on life—its record is complete (v. 6).

But while there is life, there is hope (v. 4). The lion, the mightiest of beasts, has none—for he is dead. But the dog, the despised scavenger, has hope—for he is still alive. He is able to contemplate his death, and in doing so evaluate life. Life is better than death because something is better than nothing. We must make the best of what we have now. The humanist would certainly agree with this, arguing that religion, with its promises of heaven and hell, has devalued human life. In John Lennon's words:

> Imagine there's no heaven
> It's easy if you try
> No hell below us
> Above us only sky
> Imagine all the people
> Living for today. [2]

Diversion (vv. 7-10)

Here is an uplifting diversion from the road to despair. The overriding factor is that 'God has already accepted your works' (v. 7). Michael Eaton makes an interesting observation: 'This almost Pauline touch is the nearest the Preacher came to a doctrine of justification by faith. Man has but to receive contentment as God's gift (*cf.* 3:13); God will approve of him and his works. The believer is not struggling for acceptance; he is already accepted.' [3] As we have already noted, righteousness does not come from our own labour (Rom. 6:23; Eph. 2:8-9). The works that are accepted by God are those that are the expression of thanksgiving and obedience to a God who has saved us by his grace (James 2:17-26).

For the unbeliever, these blessings are a diversion from the true eternal reality but for the believer they are a 'lay-by' on the way to heaven. He is to be thankful for temporal blessings and to enjoy them to the full. He is to eat and drink for God's glory (1 Cor. 10:31). The white garments and anointing oil were of practical significance in the hot Palestinian climate but, for the Christian, they have a deeper significance (Rev. 7:9-14; 2 Cor. 1:21-22). Enjoy your relationships, particularly with your spouse (v. 9) and be wholehearted in your work (v. 10), for these things have been appointed for you by the sovereign God for your good (Rom. 8:28).

> For the unbeliever, these blessings are a diversion from the true eternal reality but for the believer they are a 'lay-by' on the way to heaven.

Determination (vv. 11-12)

The common factors of time and chance dog all men. Things don't always go to plan. To paraphrase the Preacher's illustration: a 'lucky' goal can win a cup-tie, a 'lucky' punch can fell a champion, a financial genius can be ruined by a stock market crash and the victim may never receive compensation (v. 11).

What determines the course of our lives and the end of them? The secular man sees it as the 'luck of the draw' or 'the way the cookie crumbles'. The believer sees it differently. Luck, fate, and chance are simply the incomprehensible activities of a God who is working things to his eternal purpose. If he determines that 'the last will be first' (Matt. 20:16), and 'For to everyone who has, more will be given' (Matt. 25:29), then so be it (Rom. 8:28).

We did not determine our entrance into this world and we have no power over the time of our departure (v. 12). As the fish and birds are trapped when in the full vigour of health and activity, so is man, 'snared in an evil time'—only a heartbeat away from eternity. Man is trapped in this helpless state. His plaintive cry may well be, 'Who will deliver me from this body of death?' (Rom. 7:24).

Deliverance (vv. 13-18)

Whatever the Preacher has seen must have made a great impression upon him, for most of his journey on the road to discovering the meaning of life has immersed him in the folly of mankind. The word great sums up the magnitude of his discovery. When Moses' father-in-law, Jethro, advised him to appoint elders, it was in order that they would handle the smaller issues and Moses would be left free to deal with the greater (Exod. 18:22). Ninevah is described as 'an exceedingly great city' (Jonah 3:3). Samuel speaks of 'this great thing of which the LORD will do before your eyes' (1

Sam. 12:16). The Preacher uses the same term to describe the wisdom that he has seen—it is that impressive (v. 13). We must remember that the Preacher is writing from the perspective of Solomon, who is the wisest of men. It would take a lot to impress him!

Why does it impress him? (vv. 14-15)

This is the story of a poor man whose wisdom delivered a city from siege laid by a great army. There have been a number of attempts to identify a specific event that fits the Preacher's story: 'Archimedes saving Syracuse from the Romans by sinking their ships (212 BC), the besieging of Dor by Antiochus the Great (218 BC), and later by Antiochus VII (138 BC), the besieging of Beth-Sura by Antiochus V, the rescue of Athens by Themistocles, the besieging of Abel by Beth-maach (2 Sam. 20:15-22) and the deliverance of Thebes (Judg. 9:50-55).' Some of these, however, would exclude Solomon as the author of Ecclesiastes.

Whatever the historical event recorded, a great impression has been made on the mind of the Preacher—but not everyone is impressed, for, 'no one remembered that same poor man.' This story may be included in the passage simply to demonstrate the way people are 'under the sun', and give sound instruction to prepare us for disappointment—working for the best interest without expectation of reward. The Jewish teachers, however, later allegorized it—giving it a more overtly spiritual dimension.

A Jewish allegory

The targum of this passage—a targum is an oral paraphrase

or interpretation of the Hebrew Old Testament in Aramaic—interprets the city as a person whose body is invaded by an evil spirit. The poor wise man stands for the good but humble spirit that wages war against the evil spirit. This targum would have been used in the synagogues in the time of Jesus, to demonstrate the spiritual struggle that takes place within a person.

A Christian allegory

Although it is unlikely that the Preacher intended his story to be interpreted allegorically, we do see parallels in the gospel message of the New Testament. Man's soul is under siege by the forces of darkness (Eph. 6:12). Christ is the wise man (1 Cor. 1:30) who became poor for our sake (Phil. 2:7-8) His atoning sacrifice is God's wise way of delivering man from the city of destruction (1 Cor. 1:18-25), yet it is greeted with ingratitude (Luke 17:11-19).

The master of Christian allegory, John Bunyan, graphically writes of the siege and deliverance of the soul of man in his *Holy War*: 'Well, upon a time, there was one Diabolus, a mighty giant, made an assault upon the famous town of Mansoul, to take it and make it his own habitation.' Christ delivers the city from Satan's clutches:

> I saw Emmanuel, when he possess'd
> His town of Mansoul; and how greatly blest
> A town his gallant town of Mansoul was
> When she received his pardon, loved his laws. 4

An assessment (vv. 16-18)

The Preacher now draws his conclusions—and we can do likewise. 'Wisdom is better than strength' (v. 16). God's way is better than man's, even though it is a stumbling block to some and foolishness to others (1 Cor. 1:23). Man may despise the gospel and even try to drown out its

> Man may despise the gospel and even try to drown out its proclamation, but it should and will be heard.

proclamation, but it *should* and *will* be heard (vv. 16-17). God's wise words meet with a mixed reception. After Paul's sermon on Mars Hill, we are told that, 'Some mocked, while others said, "We will hear you again on this matter"... However, some men joined him and believed.' (Acts 17:32-34).

'Wisdom is better than weapons of war' (v. 18). George Whitefield and John and Charles Wesley often met with violent opposition as they proclaimed the gospel in the open air. Yet their message was heard above the shouts and taunts, and often turned the hearts of their most violent opponents. The Preacher's final words, 'But one sinner destroys much good' (v. 18) will form a natural link with the next chapter, but also deals with the root of the whole problem—man's sinful heart. It is through the sin of one man that we have been brought into the bondage of death, and through the obedience of another that we have been delivered (Rom. 5:12-21).

For further study ▶

FOR FURTHER STUDY

1. Examine the two great facts in our common destiny (vv. 1-6)—God's sovereignty (Isa. 48:13; 19:16; Zech. 2:9; Exod. 4:3; Ezra 7:9), and man's inability to determine his destiny (vv. 2-6, 11-12. cf. Rom. 5:12-21). Does this give you grounds for pessimism or optimism?

2. The passage deals with the reality of death as the cut off point for hope. Compare the Preacher's words with those of Jesus (Luke 16:19-31).

TO THINK ABOUT AND DISCUSS

1. What kind of hope is found in vv. 4-6?

2. Read vv. 7-10. How can we enjoy life in the shadow of death?

3. Can you see the parallel between the 'poor wise man' (v. 15) and Jesus Christ? (1 Cor. 1:18-31). What confidence does this give you in the face of your own death? How does this passage help you to counsel a friend or relative who is terminally ill and not a believer?

14 The power of foolishness

(10:1-20)

Like the most highly concentrated chemical polluting a water supply, a little foolishness contaminates and permeates every part of life. Such foolishness often parades itself across the lives of those who would claim to be the wisest and most powerful.

The Bible has a lot to say about foolishness. 'The fool has said in his heart, "There is no God."' (Ps. 14:1; 53:1). Paul speaks about the 'foolishness' of the gospel, and says, 'For the message of the cross is foolishness to those who are perishing, but to us who are being saved it is the power of God' (1 Cor. 1:18). God considered the rich man who had made no provision for eternity to be a fool (Luke 12:20). Solomon had gathered many proverbs on foolishness (cf. Prov. 10:10-14; 12:15; 15:2; 24:7) and previous chapters in Ecclesiastes have dealt with the matter (2:14-19; 5:1-4; 7:4-17). The Preacher now expands upon his conclusions—referring to the subject nine times in this section.

The main term used speaks of absurdity, stupidity and inconsistency, and the Preacher also adds fat, dull, heavy—often used as a metaphor for folly. I think we get the picture!

Its potency (vv. 1, 5-7)

The fly in the ointment (v. 1)

A football commentator makes a racist remark 'off camera'—and, although his past record is exemplary—he is finished. A television presenter chooses his words unwisely or makes an 'off the cuff' remark—he is never seen on our screens again. A politician sends a confidential memo that falls into the hands of the press—there are calls for his resignation. The list is endless. In a moment, through one act of foolishness, a career is finished. All the good that has been done in the past counts for nothing. Who remembers Richard Nixon's foreign policies in the shadow of the Watergate scandal?

The Preacher has already referred to a good name as 'precious ointment' (7:1). Now he is showing us how that good name can easily be lost. 'Dead flies' or 'flies of death' ruin the perfume. In the same way, one act of folly will ruin a lifetime's wisdom. As it is with folly, so it is with all sin. The Bible uses the picture of a little yeast in a loaf to illustrate its power. It was often used as a metaphor for corruption, ignorance, and even political guile (Matt. 16:6; 22:23-29; 22:16-21). Paul writes of its destructive power: 'Do you not know that a little leaven leavens the whole lump?' (1 Cor. 5:6; Gal. 5:9).

Foolishness in high places (vv. 5-7)

The effect of foolishness as a fly in the ointment can be seen when it is evident in high places—among those who have authority. To have a fool in your team is bad enough—but to make him team leader is a catastrophe! Thousands of young men lost their lives in the First World War when led on suicidal missions by untrained and inept officers. And to be governed by a 'foolocracy'—one dictionary even provides us with a word for it—is an unmitigated disaster for a nation.

Solomon was succeeded by his son Rehoboam, who rejected the plea from the people to lighten the load that his father, Solomon, had placed upon them—taking the advice of a group of young contemporaries rather than the sound wisdom of his elders. His decision caused a split within the nation and its ultimate downfall (1 Kings 12:13).

Ne Win ruled Burma—now Myanmar—for twenty-six years. During this time he took them from prosperity to poverty. The seven-times married dictator is said to have bathed in dolphin's blood to regain his youth. He was also known for employing a mixture of superstition and mysticism, which sometimes led to bizarre policies being introduced. His belief in numerology, for example, led him to declare in 1987 that only currency notes in 45 and 90 kyats (numbers divisible by 9, his personal lucky number) were to be legal tender, instantly wiping out the savings of millions as currencies of all other values became worthless overnight.

> To be governed by a 'foolocracy' is an unmitigated disaster for a nation.

Its pointlessness (vv. 2-4, 15)

A matter of direction (v. 2)

Man's foolishness adds to the pointlessness of life 'under the sun'. The Preacher is not making a political statement, neither is he referring to what we now know as right and left brain activity. He is simply using the perceived wisdom of his day. The right hand represented strength and protection (Ps. 16:8; Isa. 41:13) and the left hand was associated with ineptness (Judg. 3:15; 20:16) and even disfavour (Matt. 25:33). For centuries, left-handedness was considered a dubious genetic gift, and children were virtually forced into corrective measures to make the right hand predominate. Our terminology has perpetuated this: The term 'cack handed' meant clumsy as well as left-handed and, as some commentators point out, the word sinister comes from the Latin for left-handed!

The idea conveyed is that wisdom and folly are seated within the heart of a man, and it is the inclination of that heart that leads in the right or wrong direction.

No place to hide (v. 3)

In mediaeval days the jester was instantly recognized by his costume. The circus clown puts on his make up and his red nose and dons his baggy pants, leaving no one in doubt as to his role. But, says the Preacher, the fool will still be instantly recognizable without any outward embellishments—he will soon give himself away. He is a tragic/comic character, for he is unaware of the transparency of his foolishness—thinking himself wise he becomes a fool. Paul gives us this picture when he describes fallen people who, 'although they knew God, they did not glorify him as God, nor were thankful, but became futile in their thoughts, and their foolish hearts were darkened. Professing to be wise, they became fools' (Rom. 1:21-22). Modern people parade their foolishness for all to see. They proclaim a 'Post Christian' era and openly defy the commandments of God to their own temporal and eternal destruction—and consider themselves wise!

An apt illustration (v. 4)

The fool lacks self control—even in his dealings with those in authority over him. The wise man keeps a cool head when all around are losing theirs. The Preacher endorses wise advice given to courtiers in the book of Proverbs (Prov. 16:14; 27:1-3; 25:6-7)—but in this passage he is dealing with the specific situation where the king or some other official is angry with you. Foolish pride may well give us courage to respond likewise. How many of us have resigned from a well paid, secure job because we felt that the boss was unjustified in his anger? Derek Kidner puts it well when he says, 'What we are invited to notice is that rather absurd human phenomenon, the huff.' [1] The wise man, however, does the opposite. Instead of storming out, he stays and seeks to pacify his employer. It is in situations like this that the Christian is often given his best opportunity to show the grace of God to an unbeliever (Prov. 15:1; Col. 3:12-15). We are commanded to submit to authority (1 Peter 2:18-25). Jesus said, 'Blessed are the meek' (Matt. 5:5) and we must remember that meekness is not weakness but 'tamed strength'!

Its practice (vv. 8-10)

Here are five pictures that illustrate the Preacher's point. The fool must learn to be mindful of the dangers awaiting him if he does not take care—only 'wisdom brings success'. His own actions may prove to be his undoing (v. 8a). His foolishness may unleash all kinds of hidden dangers (v. 8b). He may be destroyed by the products of his own labour (v. 9)—Haman was hanged on the gallows that he had built for Mordecai (Esth. 7), and Frankenstein's monster destroyed its creator. The fool will rush headlong into a task before making adequate preparation—burning himself out in the process (v. 10). How many of us have plunged wholeheartedly into Christ's service, exhausting ourselves in his service, without first sharpening our axes in his presence (Isa. 40:29-31)?

Its publicity (vv. 11-14)

A World War II poster declared that 'Careless talk costs lives'. The fool's great publicity agent is his own tongue—he cannot bear silence. Carl Gustav Jung remarked, 'I need many days of silence to recover from the futility of words.' Or, in Paul Simon's words,

> People talking without speaking
>
> People hearing without listening. [2]

The Preacher again expands upon biblical wisdom in this matter (Prov. 10:14, 20, 32; 12:14-19; 18:21; 25:11-12). The book of James gives a strong warning against the misuse of the tongue (James 3:1-12). The 'babbler' is like an uncharmed snake and just as deadly! (v. 11).

Devouring (v. 12)

'You love all devouring words, you deceitful tongue' (Ps. 52:4). The comparison between the wise man and the fool is powerful. When a wise man speaks, the effect is positive—a fool's words lead only to destruction. The fool's speech is ungracious and will often hurt others but, in the end, they will bring greater hurt to himself. I once heard a preacher precede his sermon with the prayer, 'Lord, please make my words sweet, for I may have to eat them!' We would do well to echo his words.

Maddening (v. 13)

What begins as foolishness ends in 'raving madness'. His foolishness ceases to be an aberration and becomes a pathological condition. We can illustrate this by using depression as an example. Everyone feels depressed from time to time—circumstances, tiredness, a feeling of helplessness can weigh us down for a period. But we thankfully emerge unscathed and probably a lot wiser. But for some it has become a clinical condition. When they say, 'I am depressed', they are not describing a feeling but a state of being that has enveloped them. So it is with foolishness. What can begin as a momentary act or word can end in a state of being.

Ignorant (v. 14)

The fool mistakes quality with quantity. Jesus said this about the prayers of the unbeliever: 'But when you pray, do not use vain repetitions as the heathen do. For they think that they will be heard for their many words' (Matt. 6:7). He has no knowledge of the future but will hold forth with great confidence on the matter. He cannot speak wisely because he has no wisdom—he cannot speak truthfully for he does not know the truth for, as Jesus said, 'Out of the abundance of the heart the mouth speaks' (Matt. 12:34).

Its politics (vv. 16-20)

The Preacher now returns to folly in the national life and focuses upon four needs which have been denied to a nation by a foolish ruler.

The need for maturity (vv. 16-17)

> Immaturity in a leader is a recipe for disaster.

Immaturity in a leader is a recipe for disaster. The young leader will make up for his lack of experience by consulting with those who have more experience than him. The picture of the 'child', petulant, is contrasted with 'the son of nobles', someone who may well be as young, but who has grown into his position and has been prepared for it. The Bible speaks of the judgement of God upon immature leaders (Isa. 3:1-5), and although age is no guarantee of maturity (1 Cor. 3:1-4; Heb. 5:11-14), the church is instructed not to make hasty appointments of immature believers into office (1 Tim. 3:6).

The need for industry (v. 18)

The foolish leader feels secure and satisfied with his position without the desire to exercise the responsibility that goes with it. God's judgement may come in two ways: as a direct act for our disobedience (Acts 5:5, 10) or his permitting us to reap the consequences of our action or inaction (Rom. 1:24). In this case it is the laziness of the ruler that will allow decay. The Bible speaks of diligence in all matters, especially those relating to our service of God (1 Tim. 4:15; Heb. 6:11).

The need for prudence (v. 19)

It would appear that the Preacher is simply describing the attitude of the foolish ruler who is completely indifferent to his responsibilities. Money has become his god—a seemingly inexhaustible means of supporting his lavish lifestyle. He is indifferent to the needs of his people, and God will judge him for it (Amos 2:7; 4:1; 5:11-12).

The need for caution (v. 20)

'A little bird told me' is a saying that appears in many forms and cultures. The Preacher uses it as a word of warning to the imprudent man who thinks he will not be overheard when speaking ill of others. He goes as far as to say, 'Do not curse the king, even in your thought.' It is very difficult to harbour a thought continually without it eventually finding expression in words. Feelings of anger, resentment and criticism will eventually be expressed—sometimes bursting forth when we least expect it. It is better not to harbour such dangerous thoughts in the first place.

For further study ▶

FOR FURTHER STUDY

1. Read and consider these Bible passages on foolishness: Ps. 14:1; Prov. 10:10-14; Eccles. 2:14-19; Luke 12:13-21. How do they describe the fool?

2. A fool's tongue soon gives him away (vv. 11-14). Read James 3:1-12. How controlled is your tongue?

3. What are the key elements of leadership found in vv. 16-20?

TO THINK ABOUT AND DISCUSS

1. 'Modern man parades his foolishness for all to see.' Give examples of how he does this.

2. Examine the five pictures of foolishness in vv. 8-10. Think of instances in your own life that parallel these. What preventative steps could be taken to avoid these in future?

15 He who dares wins!

(11:1-6)

The Preacher has taught us to be cautious and to adapt our lives to fit into a world through which we are only passing. Now he invites us to take a leap of faith into what God can do—a faith and generosity that trusts completely in the sovereignty of God!

The ongoing theme of the book has been 'vanity' and 'grasping for the wind'—the futility of seeking happiness in the things which are under the sun. What is the best thing to do? Are we to remain pessimistic? The resounding answer is 'No!' In these six verses we are instructed to take the initiative.

Faith (v. 1)

My house backs on to the village pond. On a warm summer's evening you can sometimes see the soggy bread floating on the surface of the water—the ducks have had their fill, and the seagulls have grown tired of swooping and left for richer pickings. Food has now become litter. If we leap to conclusions as to what the Preacher is saying, we can be led to believe that his wheels are firmly in the rut of 'vanity'. But, in fact, he is taking the opposite approach. He is urging faith, adventure and action.

'Cast your bread upon the waters, for you will find it after many days.' How we interpret these words will not affect the overall injunction to exercise faith—but our application of them is important. The commentators are divided in the matter, but there are three main suggestions that need to be borne in mind:

Agriculture

The whole passage has an agricultural theme, and it has been suggested that the Preacher is referring to sowing the seed of the rice plant—but it is unlikely that he would have had any knowledge of that. He may be referring to the Egyptian practice of sowing 'bread corn' (Isa. 28:28) in the Nile delta when the waters were beginning to subside—leaving a loamy bed on which the 'lost' seed would be deposited.

Philanthropy

The traditional interpretation of this passage points to acts of charity. The Targum reads: 'Give your nourishing bread to the poor who go in ships upon the surface of the water, for after a period of many days you will find its reward in the world to come.' An Arabic proverb says almost exactly the same: 'Do good, cast thy bread into the water; it shall one day repay thee.' This is the picture of a person giving willingly and cheerfully without expectation of short term gain, knowing that this pleases God and will reap an ultimate harvest (2 Cor. 9:7-8; Matt. 6:19-20).

Commerce

The most common understanding is that of a merchant who is operating a fleet of ships. This would certainly point us to Solomon, 'For the king had merchant ships at sea with the fleet of Hiram. Once every three years the merchant ships came bringing gold, silver, ivory, apes and monkeys' (1 Kings 10:22). Solomon's trading in this area was a long-term investment!

Whatever picture the Preacher is trying to paint for us, the moral is the same. Michael Eaton gives a good summary when he says, '(*Cast*) demands total commitment, ... and has a forward look to it (*and you will find*), a reward which requires patience (*after many days*).' [1] Surely the Preacher is telling us to step out in faith, or, as Jesus instructed his disciples, 'launch out into the deep and let down your nets for a catch' (Luke 5:4). Our lives should be lived with this kind of boldness. In the face of the grinding reality of life under the sun we have a heavenly perspective of a God 'who is able to do exceedingly abundantly above all that we ask or think (Eph. 3:20). The Christian should be someone who is constantly 'pushing the boat out'.

George Whitefield often preached outside the courthouse in Philadelphia. On one occasion, a young man, holding a lantern, struggled through the crowd and stood near him. He became so absorbed in what he heard that the lantern fell from his grasp and crashed to the ground, disturbing the preacher and angering the crowd. The boy was acutely embarrassed. Many years later, during Whitefield's fifth trip to America, he met a prominent minister. As they talked together the minister asked Whitefiled if he remembered the incident. 'Oh yes,' said the great preacher, 'I remember it well, and have often thought I would give anything in my power to know who that little boy was, and what had become of him.' The minister replied, 'I am that little boy.'

The bread we cast upon the waters by faith may take a long time returning to us, but when it does—oh what joy!

Generosity (v. 2)

> The bread we cast upon the waters by faith may take a long time returning to us, but when it does—oh what joy!

How we apply this verse depends much on how we interpreted the previous one. It can urge generosity or caution—or both! The term 'to seven and also eight' is not to be taken literally. The use of numbers in this way was a well known tool in Hebrew literature to denote an indefinite number (Prov. 30:15-31; Amos 1:3-13; 2:4).

The farmer must scatter as much seed as widely as possible—the philanthropist must share his possessions in several ways and with as many people as possible—and the businessman is counselled to be wise in his investments, and not 'to put all his eggs in one basket'. As R. N. Whybray says, '[He] is advising readers to take the risk involved in sea-trade (v. 1), but also to spread the risk by sending the goods in separate consignments (v. 2).' [2]

The picture here is of a man who is ungrudging in his commitment—who is wholehearted in what he is doing. The Preacher's words of caution, 'For you do not know what evil will be on the earth,' should not deter us from action. If we were only to look at the pitfalls and possibilities of failure we would do nothing! Faith is not throwing caution to the wind—it is 'the substance of things hoped for, the evidence of things not seen' (Heb. 11:1). Surely this is the way we should respond to a God who commands us to trust him— the labour is ours but the return is God's. Jesus echoes this in the Parable of the Sower (Matt. 13:1-23), the Parable of the Talents (Matt. 25:14-30) and in his instruction, 'Give, and it will be given to you: good measure, pressed down, shaken together, and running over will be put into your bosom. For with the same measure that you use, it will be measured back to you' (Luke 6:38).

Providence (v. 3)

Why are we to be so wholehearted in our faith? The answer given is perfectly simple—God is in control of everything. The Preacher is drawing our attention to expected events: 'If the clouds are full of rain, they empty themselves upon the earth'—and unexpected events: 'And if a tree falls to the south or the north, in the place where the tree falls, there it shall lie.' We can see some things coming, but others take us by surprise.

The eye of faith sees things from a different perspective than the natural eye. We may all look at the same objects, but how we interpret them is another matter. One man's problem is another man's opportunity. The natural eye sees only the gathering storm and the possibility of random acts of disaster, but the eye of faith knows that even these are products of divine providence. Not one sparrow falls to the ground without his will (Matt. 10:29).

Adventure (v. 4)

The Preacher has already said that there is, 'A time to plant and a time to pluck what is planted' (3:2), but the conditions will rarely be ideal. Gazing at the effect of the wind and the darkness of the clouds will mean no sowing or reaping. The fact is, if we wait for the ideal condition we will rarely achieve anything worthwhile. We must make 'the most of every opportunity, because the days are evil' (Eph. 5:16, NIV). Speaking of his conversion, Paul refers to himself as 'one born out of due time' (1 Cor. 15:8). In other words, he was not ready when Jesus revealed himself to him. The life of faith is an adventure—taking the opportunities that God presents to us. Our timing may not be right, but his is perfect (Gal. 4:4).

Trust (vv. 5-6)

Only the God who created the wind knows how, when, and where it blows. Likewise, he is the only one who watches the growth of the child within the mother's womb. There is a lovely parallel between the Preacher's words (v. 5) and Jesus' words to Nicodemus: 'The wind blows where it wishes, and you hear the sound of it, but cannot tell where it comes from and where it goes. So is everyone who is born of the Spirit' (John 3:8). The Holy Spirit is sovereign as he moves within the hearts of men in the process of regeneration. We can only marvel and believe. As the hymn writer puts it:

I know not how the Spirit moves

Convincing men of sin

Revealing Jesus in his Word

Creating faith in him

But I know whom I have believèd

And am persuaded that he is able

To keep that which I've committed

Unto him against that day [3]

Trust calls for action (v. 6). Morning and evening may be taken literally as to denote every part of the day, or simply at all times. Timothy was told to preach the Word, 'in season and out of season' (2 Tim. 4:2). Our commitment must be wholehearted and ungrudging.

FOR FURTHER STUDY

1. Casting your bread upon the waters constitutes an act of faith. What do the following passages tell us about faith: Eph. 2:8; Heb. 11:1-7; Matt. 17:20; 13:31-32; James 2:26?

2. How would you paraphrase the Preacher's words (vv. 2-6) against the background of your own life?

TO THINK ABOUT AND DISCUSS

1. How does casting your bread upon the waters affect your relationship with God?

2. Generosity was a hallmark of the New Testament church. Read Philippians 4:10-20. Suggest three or four ways in which you can exercise your generosity.

3. What hinders believers from being generous? Suggest a number of ways how this lack of generosity may be overcome.

16 The span of life

(11:7-12:8)

The Preacher puts things into perspective by focussing upon joy and godliness—ever reminding his readers to remember God in the midst of a fleeting life.

Joy (11:7-10)

This section begins with a description of joy and happiness and moves on to provide some instruction on how it can be achieved in day-to-day experience.

Sweetness and light (vv. 7-8)

When looking to describe an idyllic scene, especially in relationships, we often use the phrase, 'All is sweetness and light'. This is similar to the Preacher's phraseology as he describes the 'good life' that God gives to man as he dwells under the sun.

The term 'light' is a common metaphor in the Old Testament, denoting God (Isa. 60:19), and his covenant blessings (Ps. 27:1; Isa. 45:7). In the New Testament, Jesus is referred to as light (John 1:4-5; 8:12; 9:5). The Preacher is using the term to show what it is to be truly alive (Job 3:20; Ps. 49:19). God created light, and saw that it was good (Gen. 1:3-4).

The sweetness of light is a direct reference to honey (Judg. 14:14). The land promised to the Israelites flowed with it (Exod. 3:8; Josh. 5:6). It is a sweetness that, as Michael Eaton points out, 'is to be savoured with enthusiasm.' [1] The Psalmist does this with God's Word, when he says, 'How sweet are your words to my taste. Sweeter than honey to my mouth!' (Ps. 119:103).

It is interesting to pause at the next phrase, in the light of all that the Preacher has previously written: 'and it is pleasant for the eyes to behold the sun.' Earlier in the book, the sun was the metaphor for labour and futility—almost mocking man with its rising and setting—as the central object of life's vanity (1:3-9; 2:11,17-22; 4:7). But here the sun is the visible source and sustainer of life on earth and the joys of its benefits are to be savoured. The farmer 'makes hay when the sun shines'—and we are to do the same. We are to be grateful to God for the joyous moments we experience in this life on earth.

Ever the realist, the Preacher inserts a note of warning (v. 8). Our earthly joys are fleeting, and we are not to forget 'the days of darkness'. His cautionary tone may be a reference to the trials and calamities we must face along the way—or he may even be referring to death, which brings our earthly joys to an end. 'All that is coming is vanity' seems to refer to the vapid nature of earthly joy rather than its meaninglessness.

These are the facts of life 'under the sun', but the Christian has another perspective. His ultimate joy is eternal—he is looking to a greater light that has risen on his life, and will never set. In Christ, there is no darkness (1 John 1:5), and in his eternal kingdom, 'The city had no need of the sun or of the moon to shine in it, for the glory of God illuminated it and the Lamb is its light' (Rev. 21:23). In Christ, our lives on earth will be abundant, yet cannot be compared to the joy that awaits us in eternity.

How to be happy (vv. 9-10)

'I remember my youth and the feeling that will never come back any more—the feeling that I could last for ever, outlast the sea, the earth, and all men; the deceitful feeling that lures us on to joys, to perils, to love, to vain effort—to death; the triumphant conviction of strength, the heat of life in the handful of dust, the glow in the heart that with every year grows dim, grows cold, grows small, and expires—and expires, too soon, too soon—before life itself.'[2] Joy must be appropriated to be appreciated.

> Youth is a time of health, vitality and opportunity, but is often frittered away in excesses.

The Preacher gives instruction—particularly to the young. Youth is a time of health, vitality and opportunity, but is often frittered away in excesses. As George Bernard Shaw once remarked, 'The trouble with youth is that it is wasted on the young.' The Preacher exhorts the young not to waste these precious years of their lives.

The term 'walk' is used in the Bible to denote the manner of one's life: We are commanded to walk in God's ways (Deut. 5:33; Ps. 1:1), blamelessly (Ps. 15:2; Prov. 2:5); in righteousness (Prov. 8:20); in understanding (Prov. 9:6); in obedience (2 John 6); in the light (1 John 1:7) and in the footsteps of faith (Rom. 4:12).

The Preacher is instructing the young person to 'walk in the ways of your heart, And in the sight of your eyes' (v. 9). Earlier in the book, he has already stated: 'Whatever my eyes desired I did not keep from them. I did not withhold my heart from any pleasure, for my heart rejoiced in all my labour' (2:10). The heart is the seat of joy and sorrow. The Preacher has already used this term to describe his quest (1:17; 3:18; 7:25). The eye is the instrument of the heart (Deut. 28:67; Jer. 22:17). What we see and how we see it will determine the whole focus of our lives. Both joy and misery have their origin in the human heart (Matt. 6). The young person is instructed to remove and put away the things that would produce evil and sorrow in his heart. True joy comes from a heart that is right with God (Matt. 5:8). The fact of God's judgement is the controlling principle of behaviour.

Godliness (12:1-8)

To 'remember' our Creator is more than simply bringing him to mind. It is a call to reverence that finds its fulfilment in v. 13, 'Fear God.' The origin of the word may well be found in the idea of pricking or piercing, that is elaborated upon in verse 11. In the midst of the confusion and despair brought about by contemplating the meaning of life 'under the sun', our focus is now directed solely heavenward. This co-relates with the words of Jesus, 'But seek first the kingdom of God and his righteousness, and all these things shall be added to you' (Matt. 6:33). There is a sense of urgency about the Preacher's command, for we are to do this 'in the days of your youth' (v. 1), and 'before the silver cord is loosed' (v. 6).

How much better it is to do this *before* we fritter away our time with meaningless pursuits, or before we meet the inevitable decline of old age. The joys associated with youth will soon fade and the sorrows and anxieties of life will remove them from our gaze, like rain clouds blotting out the great lights in the universe (v. 2).

A house of clay

There is a great movement to preserve and restore buildings of historic interest and significance. The trouble is, there are so many of them and the cost is astronomical. Each pressure group persuasively argues for their particular edifice—but there is little money available and most will simply be left to decline or be demolished. The Preacher focuses upon 'the house of flesh'—our own bodies—pointing out that decline and death are the inevitable outcome of life 'under the sun'. The picture of the body as a house or dwelling place is found elsewhere in Scripture. In the Book of Job it is referred to as a house of clay (Job 4:19), and the Paul speaks of 'our earthly house' (2 Cor. 5:1).

The Preacher's poetic view is open to interpretation (vv. 3-5). The 'keepers of the house' may well refer to the arms; the 'strong men', the legs; the 'grinders', the teeth; and the 'windows', the eyes (v. 3). Weakened by the infirmities of old age, access to the outside world becomes increasingly impaired (v. 4), and the 'sound of grinding'—possibly the younger people going about their daily work—is hardly noticeable as the hearing declines (v. 4). Sleep becomes light and fitful, and even the sound of a bird will rouse the elderly (v. 4). The 'daughters of music' could refer to the failing function of lungs and voice rendering the old person incapable of joining in the lusty singing of their youth (v. 4).

When the house was in its pomp it stood firm—echoing with the activities of its inhabitants—but those days will soon become a distant memory. As the poet, John Betjeman wrote,

> But I'm dying now and done for
>
> What on earth was all the fun for?
>
> For I'm old and ill and terrified and tight. [3]

The scene now shifts from the metaphor of a house to a general picture of old age (v. 5). The fear of falling or being jostled in the street is common. Bones are brittle and the merest stumble can spell disaster! 'When the almond tree blossoms' pictures the hair turning white. The almond tree blossoms in the midst of winter. At first, the blossoms are of a reddish hue but by the time they fall they resemble snow. 'The grasshopper is a burden' can point to the ungainly motion of the elderly, or simply refer to their weakness—even such a light thing can weigh heavily upon them. 'And desire fails' refers to the caperberry that was used as a stimulant for the appetite during the time of Solomon. This can represent the desire for food or sex—both of which may diminish with the advancing years.

All these are signs that the journey of life is drawing to its close. The 'eternal home' beckons and soon the streets, which brought fear to the elderly, will be filled with those mourning his death. Such a death is graphically described in verses 6-8. The Preacher gives us two images that describe the suddenness of the moment of our departure from this world. Although the old person has all the evidence of decay before and within him, the moment of death still takes him by surprise. The silver cord that holds the golden bowl is removed, and the bowl is damaged beyond repair—the winding gear that raised and lowered the pitcher into the well comes crashing down, shattering the pitcher. Death is as sudden as that! It is now too late to remember our Creator—we must do it before these things happen. Jesus refers to the 'signs of the times' and describes the events that precede his second advent, yet stresses that the moment will be as sudden, 'Therefore you are to be ready, for the Son of Man is coming at an hour you do not expect' (Matt. 24:42).

> The fact of death is never far from us but, for the Christian, there is the glorious hope of resurrection.

In 'under the sun' thinking, this takes us back to the original conclusion (1:2)—it is 'vanity of vanities' (v. 8). We return to the dust from which we were created. This is, as Derek Tidball puts it, 'a cruel reversal of God's intentions.' 4 The spirit of man, which was breathed into him by God, returns to its Creator (James 2:26; Luke 23:46; Acts 7:59). The fact of death is never far from us but, for the Christian, there is the glorious hope of resurrection. The Preacher has emphasized the corruptible nature of our earthly being, but has only given us half of the picture. Paul provides us with the complete picture. Through Christ's death and resurrection, the process is irrevocably reversed for the believer: 'For this corruptible must put on incorruption, and this mortal must put on immortality' (1 Cor. 15:53). The Preacher's scenario could lead us to believe that death has a sting in the tail, and victoriously swallows its victim. But Paul, again, provides the antidote, when he says, 'O Death, where is your sting? O Hades, where is your victory?' The victory is 'through our Lord Jesus Christ' and the vanity of the Preacher's conclusion is nullified, 'knowing that your labour is not in vain in the Lord' (1 Cor. 15:55-58).

FOR FURTHER STUDY

1. Joy is both temporal and eternal. How do the following passages support this statement? (Eccles. 11:7-10; Prov. 23:24-25; 2 Cor. 7:4-7; Isa. 35:8-10; Rev. 19:6-10).
2. How and why are we to remember our Creator (Job 36:24-26; Ps. 42:4-8; 103:2; 2 Tim. 2:8; 1 Cor. 11:23-26)?

TO THINK ABOUT AND DISCUSS

1. In this passage we are instructed to remember God 'now' (12:1) and 'before the silver cord is loosed' (12:6). What is your response to this? What things in modern life stand against doing this?
2. How do the Preacher's reflections on old age and death (12:1-8) encourage us to remember God? How would you present this teaching to your children, grandchildren or other young people known to you?

17 Man's chief end

(12:9-14)

The Westminster Catechism tells us that, 'Man's chief end is to glorify God and enjoy him for ever.' This is the Preacher's conclusion as he brings his journey into understanding to an end.

As he begins his conclusion of the findings in his quest for meaning and purpose in life, the Preacher makes a final statement confirming his own position in the matter. His words remind us of Paul's words to Timothy, 'All Scripture is given by inspiration of God, and is profitable for doctrine, for reproof, for correction, for instruction in righteousness, that the man of God may be complete, thoroughly equipped for every good work' (2 Tim. 3:16-17).

On its own, the Book of Ecclesiastes may present itself as a depressing, almost existential read. But as we have seen, in its place within the Bible, it is the perfect foil for those many passages that direct our focus God-ward. The Preacher's conclusion does just that, and it ends by focussing upon the one source of truth that is valid for anyone sincerely searching for the meaning of life.

The presentation of truth (vv. 9-10)

The wisdom of the Preacher is exemplified in his desire to teach. Knowledge amasses information, but wisdom interprets it and applies it for the good. In this desire, the Preacher stands alongside other 'wise men' in the Old Testament. Moses was given God's commandments so that he could impart them to the people (Deut. 6:1f). Ezra '… had prepared his heart to seek the Law of the LORD, and to do it, and to teach statutes and ordinances in Israel' (Ezra 7:10). Jehoshaphat sent the Levites to the towns and cities of Judah to teach the people the Law of the Lord (2 Chr. 17:7-9).

The Preacher has been diligent in his study. He 'pondered and sought out and set in order many proverbs'. Here is a pattern of preparation for all that are called to teach the Bible—it even contains the statutory three points! His conclusion will be the result of deep and careful thought. Not content with his own musings, he seeks out the conclusions of others and compares them with his own. When enough information is gathered, he lays it out in an orderly way (v. 9). He is not finished in his preparation, however, for he now turns his attention to the way in which he is going to present his findings to his readers. He wants his message to be pleasing, yet is not going to sacrifice truth on the altar of entertainment (v. 10). As Michael Eaton says, 'To be upright but unpleasant is to be a fool; to be pleasant but not upright is to be a charlatan.' [1]

The purpose of truth vv. 11

The words 'goads' and 'well-driven nails' serve a two-fold

purpose in describing the intent of the Preacher. The goads were sharp pointed sticks used to drive an animal in the direction required by its keeper. The purpose of the Book of Ecclesiastes is not to drive us to despair, but to shepherd us into the presence of God. The Preacher's conclusion opens our eyes to the barrenness of our landscape and directs us to the lush pastures of God's Kingdom. Like Saul of Tarsus we may 'kick against the goads' but are grateful for the temporal pain when we find ourselves securely in the fold of God (Acts 9:5).

The aim of the Preacher is to nail or screw the truth into our minds—to secure it firmly in our memory and understanding. The Psalmist says, 'Your word have I hidden in my heart, that I might not sin against you' (Ps. 119:11). We can also picture the shepherd driving in his tent pegs, making his sheepfold secure.

The truth is not simply the conclusions of a wise man—for it is 'given by one Shepherd'. Every thought, action or event recorded in the Bible is there by the express purpose of God. The Preacher's dissertation is no exception. 'Holy men of God spoke as they were moved by the Holy Spirit' (2 Peter 1:21).

The purity of truth (v. 12)

It could appear that the Preacher has now lapsed into his negative mode. But this is not the case. Here is an admonishment to heed the Shepherd's words above all the writings of man. Novelty and knowledge may often walk hand in hand, but novelty and wisdom are to be found on opposite sides of the street. People thirst for new ideas, new ways of understanding and interpreting the meaning of life. Even the most bizarre offerings will be gulped down insatiably. A new philosophy or theology will be embraced uncritically, only to be replaced a year or two later by another. Should this surprise us? It certainly does not surprise God! 'For the time will come when they will not endure sound doctrine, but according to their own desires, because they have itching ears, they will heap up for themselves teachers; and they will turn their ears away from the truth, and be turned aside to fables' (2 Tim. 4:3-4).

The conclusion (vv. 13-14)

Here is a two-fold maxim for true joy on earth and in heaven—that stresses the greatness and majesty of God, 'Fear God'—and the unchanging authority of his Word, 'And keep his commandments'. In

> Novelty and knowledge may often walk hand in hand, but novelty and wisdom are to be found on opposite sides of the street.

the end, nothing else matters, 'For this is the whole duty of man' (v. 13).

Godly fear is the beginning of wisdom (Ps. 111:10; Prov. 1:7). It is not the cowering fear of someone who has been abandoned in a meaningless life 'under the sun', but the reverent submissiveness of one who has truly found reconciliation with his Creator. As Charles Bridges puts it, 'Here we walk with our Father, humbly, acceptably, securely—looking at an offended God with terror—but at a reconciled God with reverential love. All the gracious influences on the soul—cherished under the power of the Spirit—all flow out in godly fear towards him.' [2]

Bishop Hugh Latimer was a courageous man whose fear of God superceded all other fears. This was seen in the boldness he showed in the presence of King Henry VIII. One new year's day, instead of carrying, according to the custom of that age, a rich gift to the king, he presented him with the New Testament, a leaf of which was turned down at this passage, 'Whoremongers and adulterers God will judge.' This might have cost him his life; but the king, instead of being angry, admired his courage. On one occasion, when preaching before Henry, the bishop spoke his mind very plainly, and the sermon displeased Henry. Latimer was commanded to preach again on the next Sabbath, and to make an apology for the offence he had given. After reading his text, he thus began his sermon: 'Hugh Latimer, dost thou know before whom thou art this day to speak? To the high and mighty monarch, the king's most excellent majesty, who can take away thy life if thou offendest; therefore take heed that thou speakest not a word that may displease. But then, Hugh, consider well! Dost thou not know from whom thou comest—upon whose message thou art sent? Even the great and mighty God, who is all present and able to cast thy soul into hell! Therefore take care that thou deliverest thy message faithfully.' Latimer was faithful to the end, being burned at the stake in 1555.

Throughout the book, the Preacher has majored on the problem of life and only occasionally offered a solution. Now he nails his colours to the mast. His wisdom is no match for God's—his recorded conclusions and even the secrets of his own heart will be judged by God, 'who alone is wise' (1 Tim. 1:17). It is in the keeping of God's commandments that a man knows true wisdom, and in such is the solution to the meaning and purpose of life. 'To fear the LORD your God, to walk in all his ways and to love him, to serve the LORD your God with all your heart and with all your soul' (Deut. 10:12)—this is the ultimate purpose of our being and our chief end. Jesus Christ is the Wisdom of God personified: 'And this is his commandment: that we should believe on the name of his Son Jesus Christ' (1 John 3:23).

FOR FURTHER STUDY

1. In the end, the Preacher directs us to God's Word rather than his own words. What do the following passages tell us about the trustworthiness of the Bible? (2 Tim. 3:14-17; 2 Peter 1:16-21; Isa. 55:8-11).

2. Has your study of Ecclesiastes depressed you or given you hope? Note your conclusions and give some specific references from the text of Ecclesiastes.

TO THINK ABOUT AND DISCUSS

1. What has the Preacher taught you about life? How have his conclusions changed your thinking?

2. What response does the Preacher expect from his readers (v. 13). How can you be sure that you have made such a response (1 John 3:20-23; John 3:1-18; Rom. 8:1-11)?

Endnotes

Background and summary

1. Gordon D. Fee and Douglas Stuart, *How to read the Bible for all its Worth,* Scripture Union, p.214.

Chapter 1—The Preacher

1. Derek Kidner, *The Message of Ecclesiastes,* Inter-Varsity Press, 1976, p.22.
2. Charles Bridges, *Ecclesiastes,* Banner of Truth Trust, 1992, p.5.
3. Jean-Paul Sartre, *Nausea (Monday).*
4. Tremper Longman III, *The Book of Ecclesiastes,* William B. Eerdmans, p.72.
5. Karl Marx, *Selected Works,* Vol. 2.

Chapter 2—'Tis folly to be wise'

1. William Gesenius, *Hebrew and Chaldee Lexicon,* Baker Book House, 1979, p.2446.
2. Michael Eaton, *Ecclesiastes,* Inter-Varsity Press, 1983, p.63.
3. Thomas Watson, *A Plea for the Godly,* Soli Deo Gloria, 1993, p165.
4. Gordon Keddie, *Looking for the Good Life,* Presbyterian and Reformed Publishing Company, 1991, p.21.

Chapter 3—From sense to sensuality

1. Aldous Huxley, *Do What You Will* 'Holy Face' 1929.
2. Ella Wheeler Willcox, *Solitude* Stanza 1.
3. Dylan Thomas, *Under Milk Wood.*

Chapter 4—Acquisition and acquiescence

1. E M Coiran, *A Short History of Decay,* ch. 1, Itinerary of Hate, 1949.
2. Martyn Lloyd-Jones, *The Sermon on the Mount,* Inter-Varsity Press, p.410.
3. Erich Fromm, *Escape from Freedom,* ch. 4, 1941.
4. George Wade Robinson, *Loved with everlasting love,* Hymn, stanza 2.

Chapter 5—A poem with a purpose

1. Gordon Keddie, *The Guide: Ecclesiastes,* Evangelical Press, p.73.
2. Michael Eaton, *Ecclesiastes,* Tyndale Old Testament Commentaries, Inter-Varsity Press, p.81.

Chapter 6—The crying game

1. Dag Hammerskjold, *Markings,* 'Night is Drawing Nigh', 1952.

Chapter 7—Standing in awe of God

1. Derek Tidball, *That's Life*, Inter-Varsity Press, p.72.
2. Thomas Watson, *A Puritan Golden Treasury*, Banner of Truth, p.315.
3. Otto Zockler, *Ecclesiastes*, Lange's Commentary, Zondervan, p.90.
4. Kidner, p.53.
5. *Matthew Henry Commentary*, Vol. 5 p.574.

Chapter 8—From corruption to correction

1. Roland Murphy, *Ecclesiastes*, Word Bible Commentary, Word Books, p.52.

Chapter 9—The Future: futility or faith?

1. John Calvin, *Calvin's Institutes*, MacDonald, p.153.
2. Thomas Watson *A Puritan Golden Treasury*, Banner of Truth, p.119.
3. Warren W. Wiersbe, *Be Satisfied*, Scripture Press, p.72.
4. Longman, p.176.
5. George Orwell *1984*.

Chapter 10—Words of wisdom

1. Longman, p.187.

2. Jim Winter, *Depression: a rescue plan*, Day One.
3. Eaton, p.113.

Chapter 11—Obedience to authority

1. Longman, p.214.

Chapter 12—Life's not fair, but God is good

1. Hengstenberg, Quoted in Lange's Commentary, p.122.
2. Matthew Henry, *Concise Commentary of the Whole Bible*, Moody Press, p.493.

Chapter 13—Pessimism and preparation

1. James Baldwin, *Letter from a Region in my Mind*, New Yorker, 1962.
2. John Lennon, *Imagine*, (song).
3. Eaton, p.127.
4. John Bunyan, *The Holy War*, Moody Press, pp.63, 54.

Chapter 14—The power of foolishness

1. Kidner p.89.
2. Paul Simon, *The Sound of Silence*, (song).

Chapter 15—He who dares wins

1. Eaton, p.140.

160

2. R. N. Whybray, *Ecclesiastes*, The New
Century Bible Commentary, William
B. Eerdmans, p.159.

3. Daniel Webster Whittle, *I know not
why God's wondrous grace*, (hymn).

Chapter 16—The span of life
1. Michael Eaton, p.144.
2. Joseph Conrad, *Youth*.
3. John Betjemen, *Sun and Fun*.
4. Derek Tidball, p.183.

Chapter 17—Man's chief end
1. Michael Eaton, p.154.
2. Charles Bridges, p.309.

ADDITIONAL RESOURCES

Charles Bridges, The Geneva Series of
Commentaries: *Ecclesiastes*, Banner
of Truth Trust

Michael Eaton, Tyndale Old Testament
Commentaries: *Ecclesiastes*, Inter-
Varsity Press

Gordon Keddie, *The Guide: Ecclesiastes*,
Evangelical Press

Derek Kidner, *The Message of
Ecclesiastes*, Inter-Varsity Press

Tremper Longman III, The New
International Commentary on the
Old Testament: *The Book of
Ecclesiastes*, William B. Eerdmans

OPENING UP SERIES

This fine new series is aimed at the 'average person in the church' and combines brevity, accuracy and readability with an attractive page layout. Thought-provoking questions make the books ideal for both personal or small group use.

Opening up
Philippians

Opening up
Ezekiel's visions

Opening up
1 Timothy

Opening up
Nahum

FURTHER TITLES IN PREPARATION

PLEASE CONTACT US FOR A FREE CATALOGUE email: sales@dayone.co.uk
In the United States: ☎ Toll Free:1-8–morebooks
In Canada: ☎ 519 763 0339   **www.dayone.co.uk**